LAVENDER ANNUAL

LAVENDER ANNUAL

Lavender Annual welcomes manuscripts and art work. All copy that is subsequently used is paid for. Submissions cannot be returned unless a stamped addressed envelope is attached and no responsibility is assumed for loss or damage.

Address all correspondence to:
Lavender Annual
P.O. Box 47-398
Ponsonby,
Auckland,
New Zealand.

Design: Sally Smith, Bettina Von Hassell, Miriam Saphira, & Nicola Jackson.
Cover: Miriam Saphira & Sally Smith
Printing: Interprint, Haltain St, Auckland.
Art Production: The Print Centre

ISBN 0-908780-16-8

LAVENDER ANNUAL

Compiled by Miriam Saphira

Papers Inc.
P.O. Box 47-398,
Ponsonby,
Auckland,
New Zealand.

GRAPHICS

Helen Courtney, Frontispiece, 97, 138
Willa Birch iv, 56, 74, 76, 135
Vivie 4, 102, 106, 43
Bettina Von Hassell 5, 21
Romi 23, 68, 71
Rachel 26
Evachild 36, 37, 38, 39, 63, 91, 92, 93, 94
Deanne Crawford 42, 43
Mary Moon 47, 49, 52
Lyndy McIntyre 39, 45
Juliet Bravo 58
Jude 60, 70
JR 89, 124, 127

COLLAGE

Bettina Von Hassell 6, 9,10,15,17,18,19
Miriam Saphira 84, 85, 136
Bettina & Miriam 6, 8, 12

— the crazy artist —

LAVENDER ANNUAL

Contents

PHOTOGRAPHS

Welcome

To the people who have purchased a copy to enable us to bring another collection out for our world wide community.
We aim to bring you some of the abundant lesbian talent that reflects the diversity of our lesbian lives in both the past and the present. We believe by bringing together and publishing our work we will raise the self esteem of other lesbians by being blatently visible. At a time when here in New Zealand our politicians are considering outlawing the discrimination of lesbians we believe we must stand up and be prepared to say here we are and there are heaps more of us down on the farm, in the factory, in the schools, the parliament and everywhere where there are women.

Lavender Annual is put together by a group of lesbians who want to contribute to raising the self esteem of lesbians, provide a venue for the many talents of lesbians to be expressed, and to cheer us up over the winter months in the South Pacific or for Northern readers to read on Autumn evenings. We trust with reader and contributor support Lavender Annual will be an annual event for many years to come. Opinions expressed in the pages of Lavender Annual do not necessarily represent the opinions of the group.

The Light Occupations of the Editor, Margaret Anderson, while there is nothing to edit." Drawn by Jane Heap for the Little Review, 1921.

K.G. BEACH ROAD

White misted on the window pane
I wrote the word that was her name
but my thoughts I hid like a frightened
child
in a cupboard-mind, dark and deep,
till the woman gladness of my love
was but a fraction short of dying
without the touch of hands
that spoke
the softness
of my own
so I came up your steps to your
doorway
I heard your soft laugh
in the dark
I felt your warm hand in her hair
your hunger was hot in my throat
but all I could do was stare
till the years that were lonely had
seeped
through the wine to the blush
on my cheeks
for strangers that you were I knew
familiar waves my body spoke and touched
your eyes a kindred part
unshadowed look
with no eclipse
or reason
that I care or seek
except I'm here and seduced by your woman sun
my feelings freed like children run
to gather in my power ways
Now I to my own have come.

Norma

LESBIAN DRESS

Look at her, she said, how does she walk! She looks like a man, she said, she walks like a man. Look at her.

I looked. Tight, very tight trousers moulded to her legs and bottom. Walking carelessly. Throwing her legs forward, stepping out. A woman. In a blue jersey, loose to match her eyes. Oh I looked all right. I'm looking at her, I said.

Annabel Fagan

Models: Katherine Mansfield and Winifred Bryher.

At The Pool Table

"Look at her," she said.
She was bending over the pool table. The curve at the top of her

Models: Charlotte Mew, Janet Flanner, Edna Vincent Millay and Bessie Smith.

thighs made a triangular gap at the top of her jeans. I'd been admiring it as she had potted three unders in a row. When I muttered "good shot" I did wonder whether I had been influenced by the curve.

Is that why I liked women in pants? No. Not really. I love seeing Jane wearing those baggy pants that have no shape at all. They're loose and comfortable and Jane thrusts her hands deep into the pockets. It was reminiscent of the way she thought. We had had some long, philosophical discussions about whether theories were worth writing about if they were never able to be proved one way or another.

I looked back at Jessica as she walked from the pool table. Her blouse was a soft beige - silk - it had that look of style about it and contrasted with the faded well-worn jeans. Jessica obviously didn't put on weight the way I did. On in one month and then spend six months painfully refusing all sorts of delicious dinner offerings to get rid of the excess. I'd even taken up jogging - bought a tracksuit and running shoes, not the latest trendy style, but some sturdy ones in the bargain bin that looked good as I pounded the pavement. I must admit I felt really good running around Westmere. There were so many lesbians living there now and I was able to catch my breath and the odd glass of fruit juice on my fitness rounds. Hearing the flap flap of my extra flesh brought them out on the pretext of attending gardens, letterboxes, car cleaning or lost dogs.

Ah, Jessica seemed the eternal sylph. Even her hair with its short sleek cut and plaited tail suggested speed. She had slim, long fingers which seemed to wrap right around her beer can. If I drank beer I'd never get into last year's jeans. When I complained about my wardrobe of too-tight-around-the-waist-to-be-able-to-sit-in-the-car-let-alone-drive-anywhere-trousers, Jane suggested I wear a skirt. I did have one. The interview model. If I was really desperate to get a job, the khaki tailored, never-dates skirt was taken out and pressed carefully to go with the softer untailored shirt in a pale rose to impress the interviewers. It was always a good tactic to reduce the threatening size of my shoulders by using pale pink. Then there was the other one. The skirt with the gathered waist that I had worn to the Aquarius Club once just for a laugh. Five dykes off to the boys club with two of us in skirts. We were brazenly unknickered in the height of one of those spirit of the moment 'let's take risks'. It was a great night until a gay bloke tried to pick me up. Another good reason not to wear a skirt.

"Look at her."
"No, not her. Not Jessica!"
"That one. The one in the dress!"

Miriam Saphira

Models: Katherine Mansfield and Amelia Earheart

NOSTALGIA

She leaned against the bar sending a cool stare to the group of loud laughing women entering the room. Bright earrings, coloured tights, long hair, one even wearing a dress. What was the dyke community coming to? She snorted into her beer. They're probably heterosexuals - the result of the popularization of Lesbianism through the feminist media.
Bursts of loud laughter floated sporadically across the room, disturbing her drinking rhythm. Oh, for the days of serious feminist theory groups, she sighed nostalgically.

Daisy Dyke

FELICITY FLOWERDAY

Models: Una Troubridge

She had such fluffy hair - sort of uncombed, almost wild, but the ruffled lace collar seemed to subdue the possibility of assertion and command. She didn't have a hearty laugh like her solid looking, size-10-shoed partner. Hers was a twitter, that rose up and down like seven year old Annabel practising her scales but missing out every other note. The collar was the epitome of Felicity Flowerday. It served no function. The lace wasn't even coarse so it could scratch the skin on a hot sweaty night, or remind you that you don't turn around at the movies and stare at that attractive woman in the second-to-back row. The collar was an extra. It reminded me of the dinners Felicity served. Little canapes with cottage cheese, roe and delicate slices of pickle - so slim it was hard to identify for those with agonizing allergies. She made little pastry puffs full of fluffy salmon mousse, delicious little petit fours, carrot sticks with curled frilled ends, celery too, and her radishes, all cut out into dainty little rose buds, but somehow, Felicity never got around to serving the main meal. Her collar summed her up, frivolous Felicity Flowerday.

Miriam Saphira

At The Museum

Models: Romaine Brookes and Natalie Barney

"Look at her," Moira said. Then cleared her throat self-consciously. It had come out too loud. "Over there," she lowered her voice and nodded her head the smallest bit,"over there".

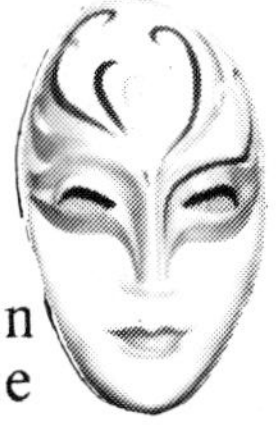

Rolly looked. "Definitely," she murmured. The woman in question looked their way and Rolly and Moira dropped their eyes to the museum map. "She saw us looking," Moira said.
"Oh, well," Rolly shrugged. "If she *is* a dyke then she'll have spotted us too."
"Maybe she's just a tourist, American."
"She's a dyke."
"But how can you really know?" Moira was puzzled.
"Sometimes I'm absolutely sure. But when I think about it, I wonder how I can be. Lots of women dress kind of butch these days."
"She's obviously not butch," said Rolly. "Anyway, neither am I. It's her hair I think. Or the way she moves."
"Well, she's not moving now. She's just standing there reading that map. Anyway, I thought she was right away, before she walked inside."
"She's wearing jeans," Rolly said dubiously, as if that wasn't it at all.
"But the little flat pointy-toed shoes," Moira objected. "And a jacket with *very* padded shoulders ..."
"Her hair's short," Rolly suggested.
"Mine's long," objected Moira.
"Well I don't know how I know." Rolly sounded exasperated. "I just do."
"I wish we could walk up and ask," said Moira.
"Wouldn't it be a wonderful world if that is all it took?"
"What's stopping you? Rolly hunched her shoulders, turned away. "I don't need to ask. I *know*."
Moira felt a stir of anger, which she repressed. Rolly was always sure of everything.

The woman in question folded her map and tucked it in the black patent shoulder bag hanging off the heavily padded shoulder of her black and white tweed jacket. She strolled across the foyer of the museum almost directly toward Rolly and Moira. Almost, but not quite. She passed them only about a foot away and they bent self-consciously over the museum floor plan. Only Moira couldn't help glancing up as she passed.
The woman in question looked sidelong, climbing steps beside them in her very padded black and white tweed jacket and tight blue jeans, her flat pointy-toed shoes clicking on the steps, her patent leather handbag swinging, her short stylish obviously not-butch hair fluffed over her forehead. And she smiled, just a small quirk of her lips upward.

Models:Margaret Anderson, Edna Vincent Millet, Jane Heap and Marlene Deitrich

Leather

"Look at her" she said, and I did.
I looked at her boots. High heels, really high, spiked heels and black leather up to her calves. I looked at her calves sliding out of her boots and her skin tight trousers and thought no-one could ever wear trousers that tight and what about yeast infections, but I didn't think about that for too long. Maybe they were tights - Moa tights, leopard skin tights but not skin, not these days, imitation more like, lycra handprinted by Julie. And there's the natural lycra now - 100% stretch cotton. Her calves really do bulge beautifully under the leopard skin. I don't know how she stays tanned all year round. When she said 'look at her' I didn't say that I've looked at her every Wednesday night for the past year, but I have, so I know about the sun tan.

She's never said 'look at her' before, and I'm surprised. After all, she's not the sort of woman you could ignore. Not easily. Maybe she's looked as well but never let on. That would be unlike her though. She's into total honesty and telling me everything. I'm a bit more choosey. I tell her most things. Anyway, I suppose it could just as easily be me.

She's got a thick black belt, it could be plastic-vinyl but it's probably leather. Like her boots. She looks like a leather sort of woman. The real thing. No cheap imitations - except for the tights but it's not easy to get leopard skin - not any more. I think she must wash her shirt in bioluval. I can't imagine her washing it. She doesn't look practical in that way. She only does the buttons up half way and you can see that her tan is all over. Her breasts never fall out. They must be quite tidy.

When she said 'look at her' she was strutting. It's true that she does strut, I think it's the heels and the way the belt pulls her in around her middle. It's quite a contrast the black belt and the white shirt, and her hair's white too. Not blonde, flattop, white. I think it shows off her tan. In fact, when the strobes are on it's quite effective seeing the shirt, the teeth and the hair.

'Look at her' I could have said but I wouldn't because she'd get upset. You're watching other women she'd say and it'd be true.

Fran Marno

Her Socks

"Look at her," she said, nudging Judy. "Look - Look at her socks." The singer wore huge workwoman's boots and thick green woolly socks. There was a lump in each sock top. "It's her lighter and cigarettes," she said, "one in each sock. Isn't it brilliant?"
"But it's not the right shape for cigarettes," Judy said, "It's not square."
"Roll-your-owns," she said.
"Of course," said Judy. The singer, called Frank, wore tights, faded and holey, screen printed with women's symbols and a black bushwoman's singlet and a thick studded leather belt.
"Of course," said Judy, " she's got no pockets."
Frank was singing a song about living on woman's land in the Blue Mountains.
"I wonder if that's why she dyes her hair blue," she said.
"Isn't it splendid!" said Judy. "But you have to be young to look like that."
"And not feel the cold?" she said.
They were both wearing the woollies that Judy's mother had knitted and identical purple scarves. They clapped loudly. "More! More!"
"Can you make out what the tattoo is?"
"Where? Where?"
"There, on her right shoulder."
"Oh, yes," Judy craned.
"Don't be so obvious!"
"It could be a rose."
"Surely not!"
"Or, no. Perhaps it's a dragon."
"Wouldn't it be marvellous to have a tat?"
"Well, why don't you then? You could always have it somewhere obscure."
"AIDS! Needles. How could you know it was a clean needle?"
"Oh, Goddess yes! I hadn't thought of that."
They looked at Frank with mingled admiration and horror. She was now singing about one woman in four being subject to sexual abuse.
"She's good, isn't she?"
"I'd love to carry my wallet in my sock."
"You'd need thicker socks."
"Right."
"And its not really my style. If I was twenty years younger?"
"Right."
They clapped and stamped their Minnie Cooper handcrafted boots.

Aorewa Mcleod.

From The Radcliffe Salon

Too Late

"Look at her," she said.
There was something about the way she sat, comfortable, at ease with herself, jeans snug, and soft leather boots on her feet. A huge, bright red jumper smothered her small body.

"Who? Look at who?"
"That one - that lovely woman there."

She was leaning back on her chair laughing, stretching out her legs and lifting up her feet in the pleasure of the joke. She leaned forward for a handful of chips. Long fingers with Egyptian rings. Soft wrist with a slim silver bracelet. Her scarf, silky, was beginning to fall from her neckline. She started to stand, unfolding like a yoga teacher and with long slow strides walked to the door. She wiped the crumbs from her hand on the back of her jeans, gave a little wave - and left.
"Which one?"
"Too late. She's gone."

Daisy Dyke

Models:Marlene Deitrich and Anais Nin

Letter Fragments

I

Dear D.
Well then, how are you now?
Are you working too hard?
Too many late nights and
you lose the habit of
sleeping: you lie there and
wander and wonder at
what you perceive in the
space of your mind. When
first waking you don't
know the fact from
the fiction of where
you have been.
I've been
reading Sam Hunt, now
I'm thinking six syllables
to the line. All the time.
I don't have to use six
I can even use seven
(sometimes if I'm lucky
it's eight).

II

I read a biography
of Alice B. Toklas.
Now I have met Gertrude Stein.
Alice was wife to her.
Gertrude Stein wrote each day and
next morning her Alice
typed it out neatly for her.
Gertrude slipped messages
into her work for Alice,
love notes in a private code,
beautifully explicit.
Gertrude's style was her own.
She ignored punctuation
and repeated words words
changing mode or meaning in
phrases overlapping
words in phrases if you get
my meaning. Later. She
discovered. The full. Stop. And
used. It. Often. So. It
was. Staccato. Not flowing
liquid lapping wavelets
overlapping in the reader's

mind voice voicing
words slowly slowly making
meaning in words in phrases
in a continuum.
I'll read more of Gertrude Stein.
In a bookshop called The
Women's Place I found some
of her work. Also a
chapter about her in
a study of certain
writers with a bright purple
cover and black title:
Lesbian Images.
I don't think I quite dare
to read that on the train
with staid local fathers
whose wives and whose daughters
I know and have camped with.

III
I wrote you a poem
last night house-sheltered while
nature breathed heavily
leaf-lashing surf-stirring
I roamed quiet mind space
gathering lines for you
in a bouquet saying
I love you.

Fran Hyland

Models: Gertrude Stein and Alice B. Toklas

Looking Good

The two women are walking with sure confident paces along the gravelled pathway, the sun scorching. The taller woman, her sunglasses covering her eyes and arched brows, is talking excitedly. Her full lips with a downward smile are reassuring the other woman. She too seems excited. As they walk she runs her ringed hand through her cut-to-bristle hair, her freckled skin with its blonde hair, glinting in the sun.

They enter the salon, the smell of perming solution, hairspray, shampoo, strikes them. The taller woman's nostrils flare. A pink smocked, highly made-up young woman greets them. Their distinctive clothing in the room full of magazine-glossied women is strangely attractive. Their excitement and enthusiasm cause the seated women to lower their magazines for a better view.
"Here's the gun, the stud goes here. It shoots straight through. That is all there is to it! Mark the spot with this."
They look closely at the shafts of metal that will soon pierce their lobes.They each mark the other's lobes.

"Who's going first?"
An interplay of banter as the blonde woman declares she will be second; she won't change her mind! The taller woman, aware of her friend's need to check the process, sits.
As she sits she is prepared for the unknown. Expectant shock of cold, and pain. The gun is placed over her lobe, the assistant brushes against her cheek. Her face clears of expression, nothing to show her tension. The noise of the operation, alarms, the sound is of scrunching bone.

The second shot makes her stomach flip, fingers flick against her cheek, the touch of flesh comforting. The studded lobes are checked. She rises, her ears pierced. Her smile slides widely over her teeth, her cheeks loose with evaporated tension. She continues to smile foolishly. She watches, her body leaning on a shampoo stand, her spirit hovering above, surveying the scene.
The blond woman takes the seat. The centre of a vortex of swirling sights, smells and sounds.

As the two women emerge to the sun they admire each other's ears. One woman reaches up, sweeping hair back from the other's ears. They strut down the road in the sure knowledge that all who pass can see the glint of metal in their proud ears.

Lynn March

AND AS FOR UNIFORMS

Can we expect a new radical approach for law enforcement agencies in the future. Here our model gives us a preview of what may come.

BUTCH & FEMME ...
1ST NIGHT
WHERE ARE YOUR BREASTS?
HANGING IN THE WARDROBE WITH YOUR SHOULDERS!
2ND NIGHT..
IS IT JUST ME OR DO YOU ALWAYS FEEL INSECURE IF YOU DON'T WEAR LEATHER?
3RD NIGHT
DOES YOUR MOTHER LIKE YOUR TATTOO?
ROMI

MOON POEM

Do you know that I watch
the moon
And remember those nights
When the glitter of a million
pearldrops
cast a path of silvering
light across the waters
and the waves sang
Trembling in our hearts

Do you know that I watch
the moon
And remember those nights
When the long dark liquid
joy
of you richly red came
fast, filling my parched throat

Do you know that I watch
the moon
And remember those nights
When we laughed and discovered
each other, silly secrets
That were the same, the same
craving for that very touch
aching for that very moment
yet promising nothing

Do you know that I watch
the moon
And remember those nights
When your skin gleamed moist
in the shadows of
our forbidden passion
while our bodies moved breathing
like one

Do you know that I watch
the moon
And remember those nights
When I clutched the flesh firm
cliff edge of your
shoulders clawing
and swung out far across
that abyss of black pleasure

Do you know that I watch
the moon
And remember those nights
When we called her down into
our veins pumping
alive in the wisdom
and craziness of our changing
selves

Do you know that I watch
the moon
And remember those nights...

Ngahuia Te Awekotuku

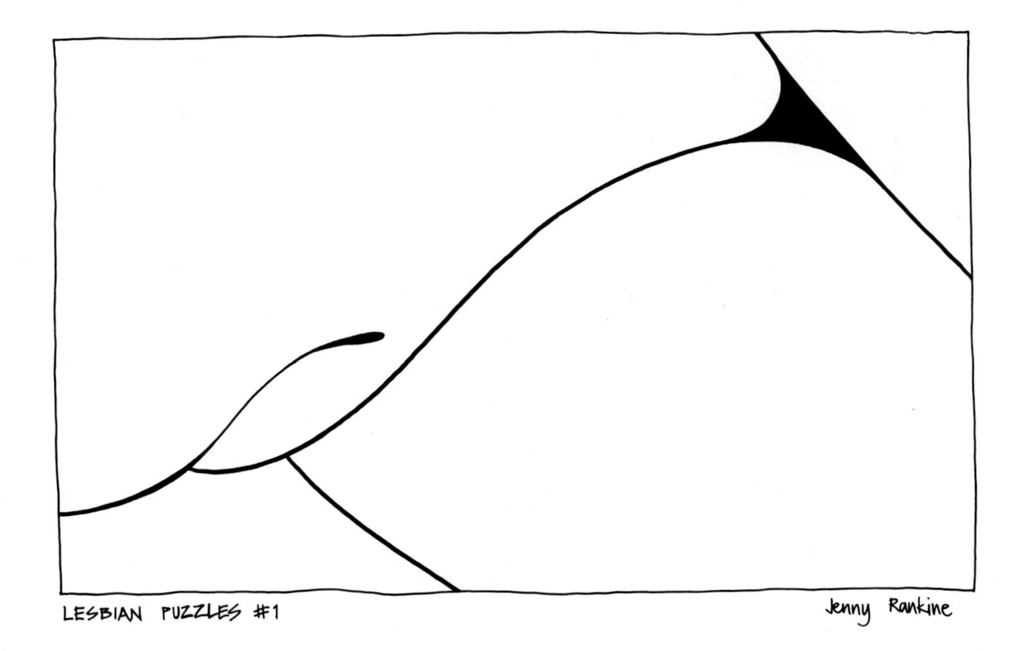

FOR THE PARENTS

AS THE NIGHTMARE CAME TODAY
THEIR SOLEMN FACES STARE THROUGH
THE TRUTH AND TEARS IN MY EYES
THE SORROW AND THE PAIN
FLOODING THROUGH THEIR VAINS
AS THEY STRAIN THEIR BRAINS
TO SEE, BUT JUST FEAR
FOR THE NIGHTMARE WILL NOT DISAPPEAR

A Not So Unusual Story

Once upon a place, a long time ago lived a little girl. This little girl was born into a very ordinary family during a time of unordinary hardships. She was born, as little girls are apt to be, with a mixture of attributes, being both extremely shy and extremely stubborn. She was also inclined towards awkwardness. Deep inside she felt awkward, all wrong somehow.

Consequently she behaved awkwardly, was quiet when other little girls were noisy and were having fun, noisy when she was supposed to be quiet. Her words would get stuck half way on the way up and come out with a d-d-d-d. And all the world perceived her as being awkward and went tut-tut-tut-tut.

Now also deep inside this little girl lived a glow, a beautiful golden glow. This was reflected on the surface by twin stars which shone out to the world through her bright blue eyes. Life is not always kind to little girls as it tries to shape them to fit the moulds imposed by men with long white beards many thousands of years ago. Family hardships prevailed. Lonely and misunderstood the little girl's awkwardness grew and grew and the lights within her eyes dimmed with pain. But the glow within never went out, nor did the stubbornness.

In time the little girl grew up through the jungle of teenage years into adulthood, became a wife and a mother. Yet, somehow she still felt all wrong and the pain and the loneliness never lessened. This made her feel quite angry at times for all her life the story books had promised her fulfillment and happiness if she devoted her time and energy to the man, the babies and the house. The glow within her burned, demanding to be felt and expressed. Eventually the man and the little girl (for in spite of her adult form, the little girl remained a little girl) parted.

Solo parenthood and financial hardships are difficult burdens for little girls, yet stubbornly she persisted. Determined to grow and improve herself, the little girl went to university and learned many important things. She joined a spiritual group and a growth group to develop her inner self. To overcome her social awkwardness and to combat loneliness she joined a community and learned how to speak her mind without fear. Yet deep within her, shyness and loneliness remained. She still felt all wrong. Happily however, when the little girl was forty years old, the beginnings of a miracle occurred. She discovered the warmth and loving vitality of women. Laughter and companionship, identity and freedom entered her life and the glow grew into a flame. The little girl discovered the adventure of her womanbody, the warmth of her breasts, the aliveness of her belly and vagina. She felt her power and her strength, which made it easier to live with her awkwardness.

One day the little girl made a very important decision. She decided to visit the home of her birth. So on a fine day she packed her strength and awkwardness into a kit bag and trudged off to the other side of the world. Maybe there she would be able to lay her awkwardness at peace.

The land of her birth was a lonely place for this little girl, as she felt the roots of her awkwardness and cried in despair. At that moment the miracle of her life came to full bloom as she looked through the curtain of her fears. Across the room she spied a twin flame, as golden and courageous as her own. Magic was in the air as the two flames drew close to one another. Breasts met breasts, bellies slid against each other, arms and legs entwined, vaginas open and pulsing, deep warm brown eyes, sparkling blue eyes. The little girl disappeared into the full fire of womanhood, able and willing to meet the equal strength of her life destiny alongside the mirror image of her soul.

Which gives this story an unusually happy ending.

Jeanne Alida

True To Your Self

Thirty years ago it was, when my Great-Grand Uncle Alex came to stay. I was only ten years old and couldn't believe that anyone could live to such an age. In retrospect he was probably less than eighty but the title of 'Great-grand' was highly impressive on the young, naive me.

I had to move into the bedroom with my sister so he could use my room. Days later, I found stray silvery hairs in there and held them out the window to blow away on the breeze. His dark baggy trousers nearly covered the sturdy high work boots with a glorious shine. His old battered suitcase (could it be older than him?) was held together by a wide leather strap with rusty buckles. I imagined it breaking and his belongings spilling out for the world to see.

He talked to us - the children - in his slow ponderous manner and he seemed too far removed from this realm to understand our interests. Ten was a carefree age of girlfriends and giggles, clubs and comic swapping. I had an autograph book (quite the rage) that was passed among my friends for the usual soppy notes - *"Roses are red"* and so on. I shyly asked this ancient visiting relation if he would write something special.
"To thine own self be true" he put above his spidery signature. What funny words, I thought and went back to re-reading *"by hook or by crook I'll be the last in this book"*.

I never saw him again or even thought of him much. Now I wonder just where he fits in our family tree. But somehow his words have stayed, even though that old autograph album has been long lost.

Haunting those words became, as I drifted through the expected life patterns: - college, work, overseas travel, engagement, marriage and children. Social pressures kept me on the narrow path of pseudo-contentment for many years. What happened?
A sudden dawning, a slow awareness, a new awakening, or a mid-life crisis? Who knows, and for what reasons, but I fell in love with an angel, someone of my own sex, and those words returned and hammered until I had to acknowledge the truth and change my life accordingly.

Dear Uncle Alex, Victorian gentleman to the core, would be shocked and horrified to be anyway implicated with my new lifestyle. Supposedly more enlightened souls have rejected me and mine. But I rejoice and embrace life more fully -share, care, and give back to the world something of what I take:- TO THINE OWN SELF BE TRUE

Jan

A Girl's Own Perennial

Jill Brame

Moira hit the top notes of the descant to *Crimond* with that air of total absorption that meant she was really watching the effect that her performance was having on Bettina, the Sports Captain. Bettina's role was one of traditional rivalry; the Sports Captain and the Head of Choir were by their roles polarized; but somehow or other Bettina's eyes kept swivelling towards Moira. Bettina tossed back a tendril of black hair from her whiter-than-white forehead. Every now and then her pony-tailed companion, Joy, the deputy, would nudge her,especially when any word such as *love* cropped up during the endless prayers that Miss Whitaker addressed to an obviously bored deity.

Along the side of the assembly hall the staff dutifully bowed their heads - Matron Nantucket, her hair Eton cropped, her beady eyes eagerly alert for any intransigence that deserved her famous cold showers; Sampson, the gangling Geography teacher, peeping through prayerful fingers at the lovely Moira; a row of neatly upholstered pedagogues.

Spotty little Cynthia, the most junior member of the choir, watched all. Her green eyes, full of dumb innocence which was her best defence against being thought of as intelligent, especially focussed on the new Phys. Ed. teacher, a striking woman with gleaming chestnut hair and lithe, strong limbs splendidly displayed in a brief culotte skirt that made Whitaker wonder about Having A Word. Instead of which, she announced the final hymn.

Miss Samuels subserviently scurried to the piano below the lectern and played the entire accompaniment gazing adoringly at the hem of Whittaker's sensible skirt.
"All creatures that on earth do dwell," carolled Moira. "Do you think the new one shaves?"
Bettina responded not missing a beat or a note. "I hope you mean her legs, forth tell?"
"If not, then let us all rejoice," came back Moira.
Cynthia steadfastly carried the harmony and the correct words. She knew her place.
"A-a-a-a-men," bleated three hundred voices, uniformly grateful that assembly had ended.

There was a scurry for positions around the new teacher. The Seniors had already heard Whitaker call her *Vicky*, which went very well with Saddler. They learnt that she was keen on hockey and swimming. They knew she had been to Our Kind Of School, and that she was a first year. Close up, they saw she did not wear make-up, and had the sort of eyelashes that bang around when they flutter.

The bell rang.
Joy and Bettina conspiratorially compared impressions in class. It was Bio. Who wants to know what's inside a worm anyway?
"She's got fuzzy knees," sighed Joy, in ecstasy.
"And a little fluff on the upper lip - it's delicious," added Bettina. She dooled Vs's all over her paper.
Joy looked slightly put out, then brightened. "She said she'd give me individual coaching in tennis," she smirked.
"Ooo," chipped in Moira, "all those hours on the volley board. I've organised private swimming lessons." She paid extravagant attention to her worm.

"What!? You've got a pool at home!"
"All the more reason," Moira luxuriated. "Do you know, I don't even think I can float?"
All three indulged in visions of increasing proximity in the pool ...

In form four social studies under the preoccupied eyes of Sampson, who was mentally devising coaching lessons for Moira in senior geography, Cynthia recorded the day's impressions in execrable French so as to defeat her snoopy peers. She wondered if there was such a word as *Sapphique*."

Morning tea in the dingy staff-room opened with a formally effusive welcome to Vicky from the Headmistress, followed by a round of tepid and compulsory applause and equally tepid and compulsory tea.

"Do make yourself at home my dear," ended the Head as she turned to the ever faithful Samuels, a tiny growth with glasses on Whitaker's left elbow. "I really don't know if I have made the right decision. All that hairiness and shorts, you know." Her eyes wandered up and down the hairiness and shorts. For quite a while, thought Samuels, thrilled at the sotto voce confidence and chagrined at the desirability of hairiness. Nantucket had cornered Vicky and was talking veruccas and cold showers.
"Nothing wrong with these girls," she announced,"except gas and pinny pains. Nothing a cold shower won't fix."
Vicky looked around for an escape route, but there wasn't one, just wall-to-wall education Realtors in sensible shoes.

In the prefects' commonroom that night there was but one topic.
"She's delectable," said Joy, "but what can she do for junior hockey? They can't hit a goal to save themselves ..."
"That'll be the acid test all right," agreed Moira, "anyway, would you believe she's got this thing about baroque music?"
"How do you know?"
Moira raised an elegant eyebrow.
"It's amazing how lonely some of these new staff feel," she said patronizingly. She was well satisfied with the impact of her action replay of a chatette about the crawl and breaststroke. Moira could make *Breaststroke* sound like the most desirable occupation in the world.
"We'd better pack up, or we'll have Samuels around. And that will be the end of special cocoas."
"What in the world does Whitaker see in that wimp?"
"Dunno - but I bet she lets her play with it!" Screams of laughter, stage hushes.
Outside the door, Cynthia stood balancing two books on her head - her punishment for reading *The Inner Game of Hockey* under the blankets. She listened to every word.

As the day of the match against St.Judes came nearer, the hockey team practised furiously. Vicky, poor woman, grabbed the occasional solitary moment to write to her mother embroidered accounts of the students' many little kindnesses - the flowers, the poems, the books carried, the keenness for individual coaching, the supportiveness of the Sport's Captain and her deputy..."But she added regretfully, there seems to be a competiveness in their acts of goodwill entirely missing from the sports field..."
Cynthia went for long runs. Her spots disappeared. She took her hockey stick down to the volleyboard to practise her shots. She was doing so with amazing vigour and accuracy when Joy came down swinging her racquet, her hair, and the bouncy bits of her body.
"Get out, you nasty little nerd." Cynthia didn't hear her. She was totally engrossed in visualizing the ball landing on an exact crack on

the board. It did.
"Out!" screamed Joy. She knew Miss Saddler was wondering why so little progress in tennis had been made. She didn't fancy Joy's swing and that hurt.
Cynthia practised another shot.
It hit the crack again.
Joy practised her swing on Cynthia.
Cynthia hit the deck.
After Nantucket had given Cynthia several cold showers, she conceded that the child was concussed and might need a little rest.

There was a grim assembly at which Whitaker ripped Joy's Deputy badge off, taking little bits of gym slip with it. Bettina's voice was all nasal and sodden, so Cynthia virtually carried the descant to *Aberystwyth* all by herself. She caught Moira glancing at her with approval. Moira had smiled at her! She glowed; she blushed; she dropped her hymnbook. Sampson gave her two hundred lines, promptly and with relish.
"What shall I write?" asked the demure Cynthia. "I must not smile at seniors?"
"Three hundred," snarled Sampson and went to console Joy.
Despite these set-backs Cynthia led the junior team against St Judes with elan, unflustered by the well-meaning cries of encouragement from Whitaker, who zoomed up and down the field like a demented chook.
It was a draw at half-time. Oranges were passed around.

During the second half, Nantucket screamed, "Kill! Kill! Kill!" at regular intervals. Bettina was hoarse from cheering. Samuels burst into the *Marseillaise* for God knows what reason. Yet none of this distracted Cynthia from swiping a mighty goal, only to turn and find herself being borne down by the biggest, meanest, beefiest, nastiest opponent that had ever had the nerve to call itself a junior and get away with it. The girl had obviously been munching steroids for years and was a direct reincarnation of Mongol hordes. "Not more cold showers," thought Cynthia, as the stick whacked and she passed out

Whistles blew.

When her eyes opened, she was being cuddled gently on the sidelines. Around her were faces which should have been anxious and well-meaning, congratulatory; but were in fact registering several degrees of astonishment ...Bettina. Whitaker and Samuels. Joy. Moira!

Then, whose arms cradled her? Whose voice murmured, "We won, my plucky little poppet, and it was all due to you"? Whose chestnut hair brushed her cheek?

She tried to focus.

Vicky Saddler pressed the ice-pack against the rising lump.

"Are you all right?" she asked, gently.

"Yes," said Cynthia, "but I think I'm going to faint."

Cryptic Crossword

Across

1. Teasing a bull he deserves ado in the tram (7)
5. Blade runs forwards and backwards (5)
8. Couples of fruit (5)
9. Three score years and ten (7)
10. The use of physical or mental energy (6)
12. Many low layers of cloud resembling fog (6)
13. They can be hired to carry a cricket team in a back street (5)
14. The French Church of England with lavender (4)

15. "It's a .... way to Tipperary" (4)
17 Pester by a dog (5)
19. Be tall and join in the dancing (6)
21. Food for the Ad. lass (5)
24. Dragster without a cross sends her love (7)
25. Saint becomes Norwegian woman (5)
26. Abominable snowmen? (5)
27. Good, bad or balance? (3,4)

Down

1. Moderate leap into a tree (5)
2 & 20. Even if it works twenty four hours a day it is not always on the go (7,5)
3 & 17. Theatre dress required for a movie (6,6)
4. A .... by any other name would smell as sweet (4)
5. Holds your attention (6)
6. Another name for Anita (5)
7 & 22. Girl sang hymn in a variation of speech used by Cockneys (7,5)
11. Home of the Magician, the Empress and the Crone (5)
12. Sings to divine portents (5)
14. First woman seen in New York (7)
16. Egg shaped primitive wind instrument
18. Parent and child make fruit (6)
23. Grey, pale and burnt as hydrocarbons contain (4)

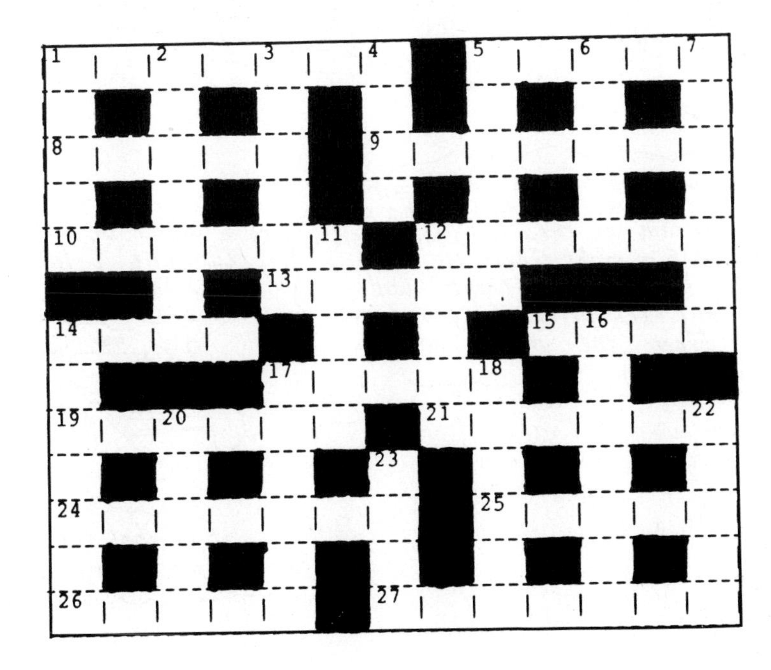

"NEGATIVE PREDICTIONS"

or

"DARE I BELIEVE SOMETHING GOOD MAY HAPPEN?"

MARIA, TRAMPING IN BUSH MILES FROM LOVER WHO IS PATIENTLY AWAITING HER ARRIVAL IN A STRANGE CITY

I bet a TORRENTIAL STORM will wash the path away and we'll all be SWEPT to our DEATHS in the valley

or a giant Kauri tree will CRACK from the impact of a SUBTERRANEAN EARTH TREMOR and fall, CRUSHING all but one of us to DEATH...

and that one will have to make a LONE STRICKEN journey back to civilisation and break the news to Jane, waiting happily and OPTIMISTICALLY for me on the hotel steps.

She won't be able to believe the horrifying news. HEARTBROKEN and UNASHAMEDLY she will cry for her woman love.. Shocked onlookers will find this passion for a person of her own sex barely credible.

or two sparrows will COLLIDE in the air hundreds of feet above, and (gathering a MURDEROUS MOMENTUM as they fall) will land – by a terrible FATE – right upon ME – their beaks (by the bad luck of CHANCE) will PLUNGE into my neck artery leaving me PARALYSED from the mouth down... .... (for life)

I won't be able to tell Jane I love her... ever again.

or that she pisses me off

or.... being in a PATRIARCHAL MALE CONTROLLED environment, I'll have nowhere to put my USED TAMPON
and will SURREPTITIOUSLY hide it in the HELICOPTER engine
which will cause ENGINE FAILURE just when we don't happen to be over the sea or a lake (1·02% chance)
jagged peaks
I MAY parachute to safety (there is a SLIM chance)
HOPE
...and return safe and sound to the city, our meeting place of LOVE
But as I walk into our hotel room I'll slip on a LOVE NOTE that Jane left for me on the WELL POLISHED Lino floor
and bruise my face badly on her SUITCASE that she left out of the way by the wall. (If only she'd bloody left it in the DOORWAY this wouldn't have happened)
I just KNOW SOMETHING will go wrong.

OI? WHAT ABOUT US?

This is a list of suggestions from Lisa Power (OLGA, London) the Secretary-General of the International Lesbian and Gay Association presented at the 9th Annual Conference at Oslo. It was based on the work of Kirsten Hearne and Dennis Killen. Although the list is not exhaustive it is a good place to start thinking about the ways we make it difficult for all lesbians to attend our events. If the organiser overlooks these things then it is our function to remind them of the difficulties some of us have getting access to activities we would like to attend.

Contacts

* Are there any lesbian differently-abled groups or networks in your area that you can contact and talk with?

* Are there groups for differently-abled groups that you can publicize your newsletters and events? Try the radical groups first and then the mainstream groups. It may come as a bit of a shock to them when they realise that lesbians are everywhere.

Information.

* Is your newsletter/discussion paper/agenda on tape?

* Are your notices in LARGE TYPE?

* Have you considered putting your information in Braille? (Though some organisations prefer tapes)

* Do you send press releases to the disability media? In England during the Section 28 debate there were special showings of televised debates with signer and subtitles due to the pressure from the gay and lesbian community.

Access to events

1. Can someone in a wheelchair attend your meeting/ event? You may think you are butch enough to carry one but some electronic chairs weigh up to 400lbs. Also the person in the chair may not be so keen on the risk of being dropped, hurting some-one's back or being made a fuss about. If they can get in can they also get to the toilet? Are the internal doors wide enough?

2. Do you have a signer for deaf people? Do you know how to find a signer if one is requested?

3. What are the arrangements for smokers? Now that there are more smoke free areas are the smoking areas well defined enabling smokers to get to them easily? Making a smoking area in a corridor makes it difficult for both groups because people with breathing difficulties may have difficulty negotiating the walkway. Where smoking is allowed at an event have you asked no more than one person at a time to smoke?

4. Did you know that strobe lighting can cause fits in epileptic people and headaches and nausea in people with eye damage?

5.Do you know of buildings with Link systems for the hard of hearing?

6. Do you have regular breaks with drinks and preferably some sort of food available? It may sound obvious, but sometimes events become endurance tests which cause problems for diabetics, hypoglycaemics, and others.

7. Will a guide dog be allowed to go wherever you meet?

Hidden Disbilities

Did you know that not all disbilities are obvious? Someone with a dietary, breathing, mental or other difference may not be at all noticeable except that they may be absent from your event if their needs have not been met. Also, many people's difference affects their level of stamina. Do you wait to have this pointed out or do you take into account when you are planning?
It can be just as easy to spell a name slowly twice or say a telephone number slowly, than to rattle it off too fast and wonder why the person never called you up.
It can be easy to explain at a party that you will keep the music down for the first two hours so that people with difficulties with loud music can come and enjoy the event before it is too raucous.

Language

I've left this to the end deliberately, because though it is important, it is pointless to change our language about disability without changing the material conditions. Too often we learn to use right-on phrases

about race, sex, and ability without examining the underlying practicalities. Language that degrades or trivialises differently abled people is best avoided. Do you talk about people being 'blind to the facts', 'completely insane', 'dumb', 'an emotional cripple', 'blind as a bat', and 'mute as a mackerel'.
Do you talk about it 'falling on deaf ears', 'the blind leading the blind' and that anti-gay sentiment being 'a cancer on humanity'. So do we all - but do we have to?

Attitude

Many differently abled people say that their biggest problem is the way other people treat them. Feeling sorry for someone, feeling embarrassed about asking if you can help or how they are, or letting your fears get in the way of their lives is not productive to you or them. This is particularly so for people with life threatening illness. Why do you feel free to mix publicly when you have an infectious cold or flu, when these can spell the risk of pneumonia for a differently abled person.
People often find excuses not to do anything about the above suggestions. Your defensiveness may be an opportunity to confront your own fears of loss of ability. Yes, signers are expensive - so why doesn't someone from your group learn to sign (apart from the obvious benefits, it's also the only way to have a conversation in a disco). Most of the above suggestions are workable if you want them to be. Do you?

A Day In The Life Of - Saj

Saj, 55 years old, (well just about). Mother, grandmother, lesbian. The smell of paint pervades my whole life. I have pails of pale green paint. Pails of dark green paint. Cans of white, and a can of black. Ten years ago, when I was 45, I painted the house. Then I chose brown, red, green and white. This year it was time for a change. For the last 8 weeks this task has dominated my whole life. I have had no time to write, hardly time to think about anything else except what I would do the next day. The roof is finally finished, thanks to the timely intervention of two young dykes. However, when they were up there they discovered that my cold water holding tank was leaking, consequently that part of the roof could not get painted until a new tank was installed. Also after the roof was painted it decided to leak in two places the first time it rained. I am also painting the back porch, stripping and filling in the dining room prior to papering (a winter job) and had to paint around a new window I have had installed in there. I have really painted the house three times as I have put three coats on it. This was because I was trying to cover dark brown with pale green.

SUNDAY: I rose at 8 am, fed the cats and the dog. Made a hot drink. Put on the washing. Had a bath and once more pulled on my painting pants and T-shirt. Put third coat on the white in the back porch. Pegged out the washing. Had lunch. Found my tube of gunk with which one repairs leaks and shakily crawled up onto the roof. Filled in around the iron from where I hope the leaks were originating. While I was up there, decided I might as well finish painting the area that had been left because of the leaking tank. Down from the roof, put on casserole for tea. Then decided to put first coat of white around the outside, exterior, new window. By this stage I was totally buggered.

Reprieve came in the form of a visit from young dyke, (one of the roof painters). Luckily had some cold beers in the fridge. Had a few bottles, a bite to eat, then went visiting a few friends, to get away from the house for a while. More beers with them. Home to watch T.V. then crashed out in my bed.
Wielding a paint brush one picks up a sort of rhythm, momentum. Hence "Dyke Power Rap".

Dyke Power Rap

Who can you trust
when you start a new thrust
of female intervention
female intention
feminism moves
feminism grooves
but it's Dyke Power
that's who
who takes all the crap
singing this rap
for Dyke power.
We're first in the news
first with the blues
when feminism screws
our ideas up
who takes the blame
who takes the shame
Dyke Power.
Now I'm telling you loud
I'm telling you clear
so you'd better listen
you'd better fear
the revolution's happened
the revolution's here
if you wnat to scream
if you want to cuss
Dyke Power, That's us.
Now we've fought all your fights
gaining wimmin's rights
who gave you back
the past you lost
who paid the price
who paid the cost
your art and music
wimmin's writing
hear me well
'cause I'm skiting
it was Dyke Power.
When we broke male rule
over wimmin's choices
did you ever
raise your voices
for Dyke Power
and when we'd won
and the work was done

who was it that was
ostracised, criticized,
Dyke Power
it fits
that's the way
it's always been
to do all the work
but never be seen
but if we ever
come out swinging
you'd better duck
don't push your luck
with Dyke Power.
We're telling you loud
singing strong
you knew it was us
all along
we're Dyke Power.
Dyke Power
that's what you need
Dyke Power
that's what we've got
Dyke Power
it's going to cost you a lot.
Now sisters give us credit
where credit's due
we've worked very hard
we did it for you
could you ever
have made it through
without our
Dyke Power
Now we have all got different
points of view
what I've said in this rap
is not really new
there's quite a lot more
that I could say
but *I'm* getting tired
so I'll hand it away
to DYKE POWER.

Saj

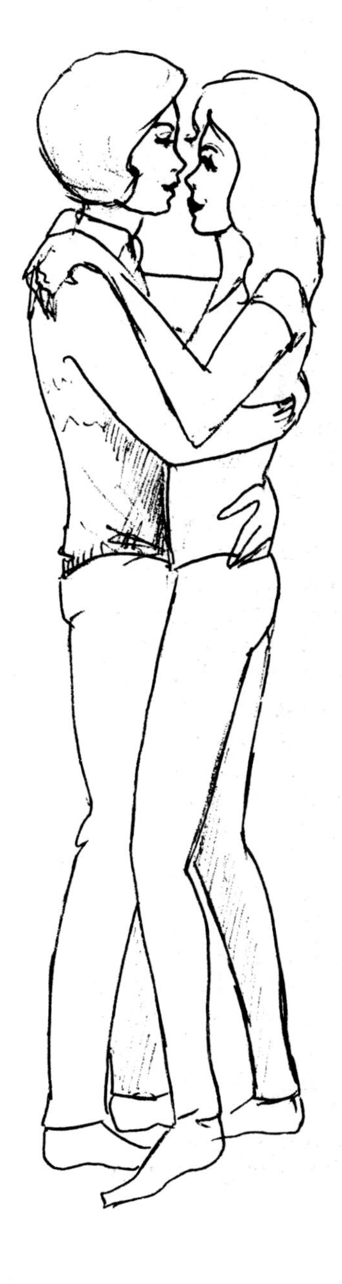

COPING TECHNIQUES
What are you doing?
If I tell you you'll think I'm mad
No, I won't
Well This is my new technique for coping with feelings of PANIC.
You see, whenever my lover is late home I feel myself panicing that she's having another affair so... I pull a paper bag over my head...
This technique allows me to breathe in my own air until the proper balance of carbondioxide and oxygen has been reached...
...This balance is scientifically proven to ease one's feelings of PANIC. See... watch!...
I think you're mad.
Evachild

What's In A Name

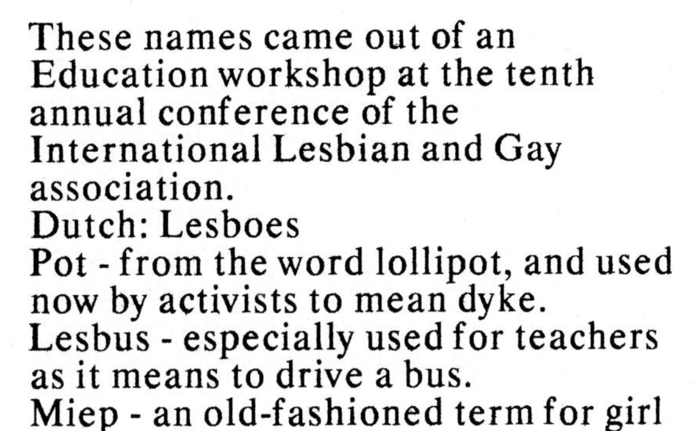

These names came out of an Education workshop at the tenth annual conference of the International Lesbian and Gay association.

Dutch: Lesboes
Pot - from the word lollipot, and used now by activists to mean dyke.
Lesbus - especially used for teachers as it means to drive a bus.
Miep - an old-fashioned term for girl

German: Schule Sau - queer woman
Kesservater - masculine lesbian
Lesber - used by men who like watching lesbians

Norwegian: Rompis - likes bums
(more often used by gay men)

Swedish: Bog - queer
Fjolla Eff - very effeminite and used for both men and women
Pugga - a small grey insect which lives under stones!
Flata - lesbian, means flat-chested
Lebba - lesbian
Truckis - means truck driver and used for lesbians.

Spanish: Tortillera - used for lesbians
Bollera - lesbian
Chapero - truck driver girl
Puton - a big bitch applied to both men and women
Marimacho - butch lesbian
Conchona - coward (lesbian/gay)

English: Queer, lezzie, bull-dyke, bus-driver and the purple people.
Did you know that bull-dagger/dyke comes from the Old English of Queen Boadicea?

Naming

Lynn March

Mary-Clare. Mary-Clare. Mary-Clare.
She walked down the clear varnished floor of the sunlit corridor. Her body moving in an unheard rhythm. Her head turning slightly towards her left shoulder, chin tucked towards her collarbone. Her eyes downcast, glanced upwards as her stride carried her past the Virgin's statue. Her lips pursed suggesting a severity which was only denied by the crinkles that gathered where her lip corners met the wrinkle creases. Her inner thrumming, to a classical piece with trumpets thrilling, not at all religious-like, was accompanied by the refrain: Mary-Clare, Mary-Clare, Mary-Clare.

When, years ago, she had knelt as Mary-Clare and risen Sister Timothy, she had cherished her name, a symbol of her newness, her shedding of worldliness. A concrete sign of the alteration she had craved in her deepest being; "an outer and visible sign of an inner grace".
She had stilled the startled cry that rose in her throat. She had 'fancied' Donna, Beatrice, Ursula, a saint, she had not considered a male name. She. So full of her female sacrifice, Bride of Christ.

She had come to be familiar with her name, to smile at the fancy of the young Timothy who had taken the name as a divine lesson for the one who had so coveted her femininity. To be a 'Timothy' was indeed a challenge.

Ten years later, Sister Francis, whose clear creased eyes would worry for her when she spoke with troubled serious thoughts, fears for her work, her lack, her inadequacy, ten years of Sister Timothy then one day a great shout from Sister Francis,
"Hello Tim, it's grand to see you!"
TIM! her heart squeezed, the shaft of joy was a hot burning spear of sun. She squeezed the arm and hand of Sister Francis, she laughed. She laughed at herself, Sister Timothy, so grand, so devout, so serious. As Tim, she felt light, bubbly, gay. Of the many gifts loving Sister Francis had given this was the greatest. Sister Timothy, now Sister Tim enjoyed herself, her spirit was lifted, her soul full, plumped with happiness.

It was with some regret that she envisioned herself losing her name of 'Tim'. No regrets for shrugging off 'Timothy' but the loss of 'Tim' did give a pang. The new order, which allowed nuns to resume their birth names had been a surprise. She had forgotten herself as a 'Mary-Clare', forgotten how it sounded and indeed it sounded strange from her own lips. She couldn't imagine responding to Sister Mary-Clare.

As she approached her room she hesitated in her thoughts, how would Sister Mary-Clare sound from Sister Francis? She had known from first hearing the change of orders that she would resume her 'Mary-Clare', it was right for her. Many aspects of rightness were not comfortable, she nodded emphatically to herself. She would miss Tim though.

Deep in self-talk, she had not noticed the woman waiting in the corridor. Sister Francis stepped forward: "Welcome, Sister Mary-Clare." Her eye creases wore their worried look, "I wanted to be the first to greet you, Mary-Clare."

It sounded fine, her stomach muscles relaxed, it sounded fine! Mary-Clare linked her arm through that of Francis, "Let's walk".
They talked, as always. They talked of their day, challenges, worries, possibilities. They talked of the 'new' names. How some suited so well, others seemed surprising. All the resumed names had a comfortable fit, the nuns had spoken with surprise at the ease of forgetting well-worn religious names, when the assuming of them had been significant.
The writing of one's former name in a moment of thoughtlessness was an experience many had shared, some after twenty or more years.
Mary-Clare did not speak her own thoughts about 'Timothy' or her regret for 'Tim'. Sister Francis was not resuming her birth-name and had not offered it to Mary-Clare. Mary-Clare was hesitant to suggest what could become a familiarity between them.
As they re-entered the house Sister Francis stopped and turning, quietly asked,
"May I still call you Tim?"
Mary-Clare felt the lift of her heart and her cheeks to a smile.

"Hear me" by Mary Moon

TALKING BEDS BELOVED

I haven't got a double -
can I love you on a single?
mattress? on the floor? on
seagrass matting? sponge rubber
too, not inner sprung - but
we've tasted them between us,
inner springs... the current's
rich. Let's make a bed!
a startling bed, a garden bed -
        a violet bed
        a daisy bed
        that *busy Lizzie*
                naked lady
                sage
with a border of forget-me-nots,
a gladioli head, flag iris eyes -
nasturtiums to nibble absently
and chives, St Joan's wort alongside ...

a sweet groundcover, verbena?
blanket flowers for chills ...
a flame tree to fire wintry
solstices and overhead, virgin's
bower - like Artemis we boycott men -
and queen of the night outside.
We'll cultivate - among the pinks,
mother-in-law's tongue, mother of
millions licks, chrysanthemums ...
but let's leave love-lies-bleeding
till full moon. Keep salvia handy
though, and fish-tail palm
for mermaid days, and pansies,
pulses, lotus and heart's ease ...
a crane's bill to carry alphabets,
schizanthus for artistry -
Amazon root for flighty nights?
fiddlewood for the blind ...

to transfix bigots - kaka beak!
rue, their evil eyes. For us,
our foremothers' garlic heals,
and koromiko, fern - and bay ...

don't forget the loveage and silly
birds of paradise! Artemisia keep
us lusty, elder brings out the witch
and lavendar, cronies ... oh,
a riotous bed, a bedlam spell!

once planted, we might well
extend - stock, golden shower,
apples - dwarf; for privacy
coloured wallflowers and a creeper
to coil peep holes up, a climbing
fig, maybe, a vine, for times
contemplative to *trace those*

tantalising intricacies of purple
passion flowers, and thyme and thyme ...

we needn't move for days, nights,
weeks ... at all! scatter hen and
chicken, pennyroyal? to amplify,
not quicken - breath does that
with touch, more touch ... yes,
honesty, how else feed love? but
not thrift here, we've had too much
and love's luxurious - fat!
and grows, and blooms, and roses ...

we want the lot a garden goddess
offers - cornucopious wit,
prolific blossoming, buds, sprays
and frothy nosegays, flaunting
fountains and bouquets - figures
bellying seismologists'
columns we'll breed Otherworlds,
combustibly, past angel's trumpet
blasts - we have! we've done it!

any bed - single, double, queen -
sponge rubber or five finger sponge -
all's one to us riding the petals
juicily
wet-suited, bursting
thirteen dimensions off the world's
edge slip a delicate lover learns,
depth-sounding, filaments bulbous,
cast-off roles, pasts, properlies
sunk into hot compost - to find

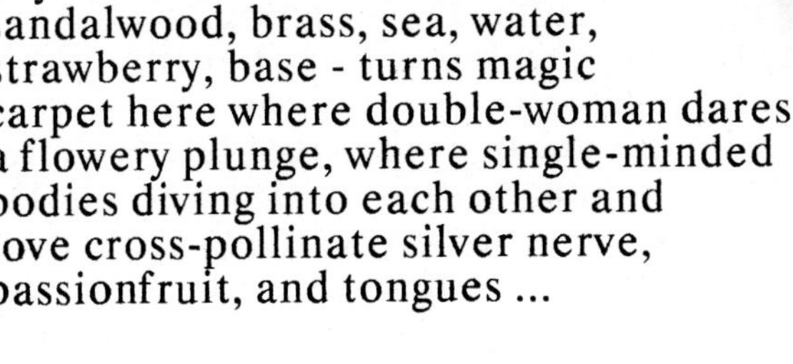
precipitance on arrival - and
any old bedrock - boxwood,
sandalwood, brass, sea, water,
strawberry, base - turns magic
carpet here where double-woman dares
a flowery plunge, where single-minded
bodies diving into each other and
love cross-pollinate silver nerve,
passionfruit, and tongues ...

Heather McPherson

FIVE MONTHS

Helen Brabazon

The sun was up. I got off the New York flight with sore dry eyes. She picked me up in the van at Victoria Station. It was colder in London than New York but there were daffodils and cherry trees.

I felt relaxed with her straight away. I was whisked off to a boring party that night. We ate raspberry cheesecake and got drunk. We danced and didn't give a damn about boring people. We grooved along with the reggae and danced outside on the pedestrian crossing with some black boys. Then home at three in the morning. The big bed felt huge with just two pillows for company. I wondered what it would be like in the flat when there was just she and I.

I feel attracted to her. Can I believe this? Is this because I want her, or I need someone? A burning sexual attraction to a woman? Such curiosity. I don't know. I'd love to go to bed with her. But do you think I'd ever tell her? No. I'm frightened of rejection, of repulsion. I wonder if I'll sort this out eventually. I feel so turned on, but more than that, I just want a cuddle - someone to hold close and snuggle up to.
We talked way into the night. I really wanted to tell her, for it to be different. So she could hold me.
After breakfast on a beautiful sunny day we went to Windsor. I just love the Electric Light Orchestra tape. It's the electric cello. How did I live without it?

The Queen wasn't at home in her castle. It was so good seeing things through her eyes - much more fun than sightseeing alone. Over the bridge to Eton - in the chapel the sun filtered through a rainbow into the grey stones, bringing them to life. Then down to Camden Town for Greek food and retsina. That sheep yoghurt is delicious. I think I love Greece already!

More long whispers with her far into the night. It's amazing.
She can really draw me out. I say far more to her than I ever thought I could. I have so many things I want to say.
She and I talked again. Somehow I can't get over the final barrier and talk about lesbianism, except in very general terms. Like we both asked each other if we had ever had any such experience. No. For both of us. But both of us are interested in the topic.
I don't understand these feelings that I have. Or why I have them. And they are not that strong that I can't put them right away if I have to.

She's a special treat. I hope she knows I'd like to say all the things

that I write down here, but I'm inhibited. I don't want her anger or disgust so her indifference is better than both of those. It's safe.
We talked - me on, not in, her bed, till very very late, early daytime! She had a baby when she was about twenty. We talked all about that. I felt very close and very special to be told.

I don't think that I can just forget about impressions I make on other people, and not care what they think.
We didn't go anywhere. So cruisy. And pleasant. And long lasting. And relaxing. And good - listening to music. I'm really aware of her. I wonder if she knows.

We just watched the sky grow dark. And I gave her a massage. I really enjoyed doing it. My fingers were talking, saying what I am afraid to say. And I know that she was really turned on. I don't think I'd ever take the initiative and, if she did, (or anyone else), I wonder how I would truly react. I can only speculate. I would have loved to have slept with her in the big bed. Back to the teddy bear!

I guess she's very mature at dealing with her feelings; knows what causes them, and goes right out to do something about it. She teaches me a lot. I can't bullshit with her. She doesn't let me. Those eyes! Does she know how I feel?

She gave me a great big hug in bed. I couldn't believe how brilliant it made me feel. So right. If only I could tell her. Maybe soon.
I was close to telling her last night. Why didn't I? What am I afraid of? Her rejection - that's what. Maybe I'm wishing she would reciprocate the way I feel - and yet, if she did, how complicated it would all be. I don't know.

My first big concert; Midsummers day at Knebworth, with sixty thousand people. The crowd held hands for "Stay With Me". Lying in the sun and the wind and the dirt and people and smokes. Food, dogs, kites, the trees and the stately home. This could only be England. The incredible sensations with the sound of Genesis, and the visuals. And her.

Does anyone love me besides my parents and the kids? I mean Love. There are lots of ads for encounter groups in "Time Out" - even here in Highgate.
I woke her last night when I got home from dinner. Somehow in the next while she came to my bed. It was brilliant. Not sexual, but highly sensual. The special talks and just being touched.

Now I look forward to going to bed! And I sleep perfectly.
I want sex.
So here's the seventh month of the year and nobody cares about me to distraction.

These days I can't put the feelings away any more.
In bed with her I finally finally told her how I feel about her. And it was marvellous. She was so nice. Big hugs and listening, and telling me it was all right and normal and she didn't feel bad or hate me. I can't describe the relief. We talked for hours, touching each other gently. I felt brilliant; so glad to be alive. There was nowhere else in the world I wanted to be than with that woman, safe and sound.

She woke me with tea and no mention of last night. But I guess there's an extra special understanding now. She knows - it's all right!

It felt so good last night to be able to touch her. And to be held in her arms. I didn't even want to move, let alone get up. Maybe it was a dream. All I wanted to do was to get home. All I wanted was another hug. Not just nothing. I thought over and over again about it, all day at work. I wonder if she's thought about me today. And how will it be tonight? - whether she still thinks, or not, that it's okay for me to be like this.

Well, it was okay. Both of us were ultra tired. I got my hug! Such a delicious feeling to snuggle up to her and go to sleep like that. She's back. She looks radiant. I like her so much.
I love her drawly casual voice and the confidential tone, as if she is talking to me and nobody else.
We're such good buddies. I can hardly imagine a time I didn't know her.

I find it incredibly hard not to want to touch her and be held, at night especially. I guess I've got her right out of perspective. What does she really think about me?
We want to travel in the van. If only I could get rid of my extra feelings towards her. They get in the way.
I'm beginning to believe that it is really happening - this van trip.
I'm lonely for a lover.

We cleaned the flat and packed. Off on our adventure to the sun. We found a campsite at Ramsgate. It was too late to contemplate arriving in France in the dark.
She and I slept in the van - the others were in the tent. Calais - and the right side of the road. Marc Chagalls's blue green windows at Reims. Bonjour!
Guns, guards, borders - into very neat, highly developed Germany. Window boxes and big houses with apple orchards.
Austria and a pink sunset on the peaks. Bells and barns. Yugoslavia and lemon icecream. Exploring the world - with her. I'd like us to go to the Bahamas next.

Another epic night. Watermelon feasts and delicious hugs. It's so divine to be held tight and cared about. She tries to understand. I stay awake a lot but I don't care, even at sunrise!
I watched her sleeping close to me, with one hand under her chin. She looked really lovely - such long eyelashes; her face all soft and relaxed. I wished she'd stay asleep for hours so it wouldn't be disturbed.

Eventually we got to Greece. Poverty and dust, but smiling laughing and friendly people. There are chickens all over the road! Sheep yoghurt and cherries the size of plums. And huge peaches. So I'm twenty-three. I'm in love with her.

The olive trees are silvery, like pohutukawas. She gives me figs in bed. And peaches. Theres something in the air in Greece. I really want to make love.

I don't know what to say at first. We are lovers.

How can taking your clothes off feel so wild? - let alone anything else! She encouraged me to explore her - such a tremendous turn-on for me. But more than the physical aspects was the emotional thing of doing something about how I felt. And it was okay with her. It felt just brilliant. I never wanted the night to end. No bullshitting. I felt great. It was slow and hilarious at times. Neither of us knew what to do! But gradually we broke down all the barriers and made love. It's one of the most special things that has ever happened to me. I won't be sorry. At last my curiosity has a few answers. Ever time I think of it I feel turned on. It's that sort of flash; of intense feeling at ovary level. It's a special secret. What a waste this took us five months.

TO HUG OR NOT TO HUG...
Oh well.... Goodbye then see you Friday!
Yeah. Goodbye!
God... do I hug her or not?
oh dear, have we known eachother long enough to hug eachother?
Well...., ah... Friday then...
Yeah.... ...see you then
HUG
SQUEEZE
Oh, I wonder if she thinks I'm "doing a line" sexually...
Oh I hope she doesn't think I want to have a relationship with her!
am I?
Do I?

Evachild

Ex Marks The Spot:
A Guide To Lesbian Cultural Festivals

Meeting the Ex-Lover At The Pool Table

I What to say:

From previous experiences, these are the adages that other lovers have given me for meeting with the Immediate Ex:
1) Don't talk about religion, politics, and especially don't talk about the Springbok Tour, and don't use big words.
2) Don't talk about the cleaning lady you met the other morning.
3) Don't talk about the children, or about Lesbianism.
4) Don't talk about <u>us</u>.

Perhaps my next lover will suggest:
5) Don't talk. For goodness sake pretend you've had your jaws wired, are stone deaf, or don't speak English so good - only small- small. However it is permissible to say, "Hello."
N.B: It is <u>very important</u> to follow this up with the Right Name.

II What to wear

1) Avoid colour coordinating with your lover. It's tacky.
2) Attempt to wear very long sleeves over any tattoo which may give rise to comment.
3) If bruised and bitten, wear a polo neck.
4) Make very certain that you know exactly where you got every one of your rings from.
5) It is advisable to suss out the dress code in advance. The flowing flowery stuff will make you feel just a little insecure in a room full of heavy denim and black leather.
6) Wear something.

III Behaviours to avoid with your lover during the course of the evening: (according to the Ex.)

1) Physical contact
2) Eye contact
3) Full frontal contact
4) Breathing

IV Situations fraught with danger:(i.e. those situations which should make you move away, saying quietly:"I must go to the loo," "What a lovely view from the front door - I must go look at it again..." or preferably nothing, so conserve energy to move away faster.)

1) Any situation involving kitchen activities. (There's a lot of murder weapons in the kitchen.)
2) Any situation involving your admiration of an object which your lover may have given to your ex.
(Wedgewood and stuff is unbelievably fragile but leaves awful bruises.)
3) Any move to look at photographs or albums.
4) Any situation involving well-worn records or tapes. Apparently the Accident & Emergency Department now have a much better system for removing these things from people's mouths, nostrils, etc; but you do need expert help.)

V Beverages:

You either need to be a) stone cold sober throughout or b) entirely out of your tree. a) is excellent if you plan on moving away quickly, but b) excuses any aberrant behaviours and means you are totally, but TOTALLY relaxed.

VI Strategies and Tactics

1) If there is verbal unpleasantness, the following is not a good strategy:
"You know, another woman I know had someone say that to her, 'n' y'know what she said back? 'You bloody bitch,' that's what she said."
Stuff like that leaves the other person feeling not OK, for some reason or other, and IS less likely to promote a gracious and ongoing warmth....
2) ALWAYS hang on to the car keys. You may find that your lover and her ex have some small matters to discuss further. It can help if you can drive to Taupo or Wellington while they do that.

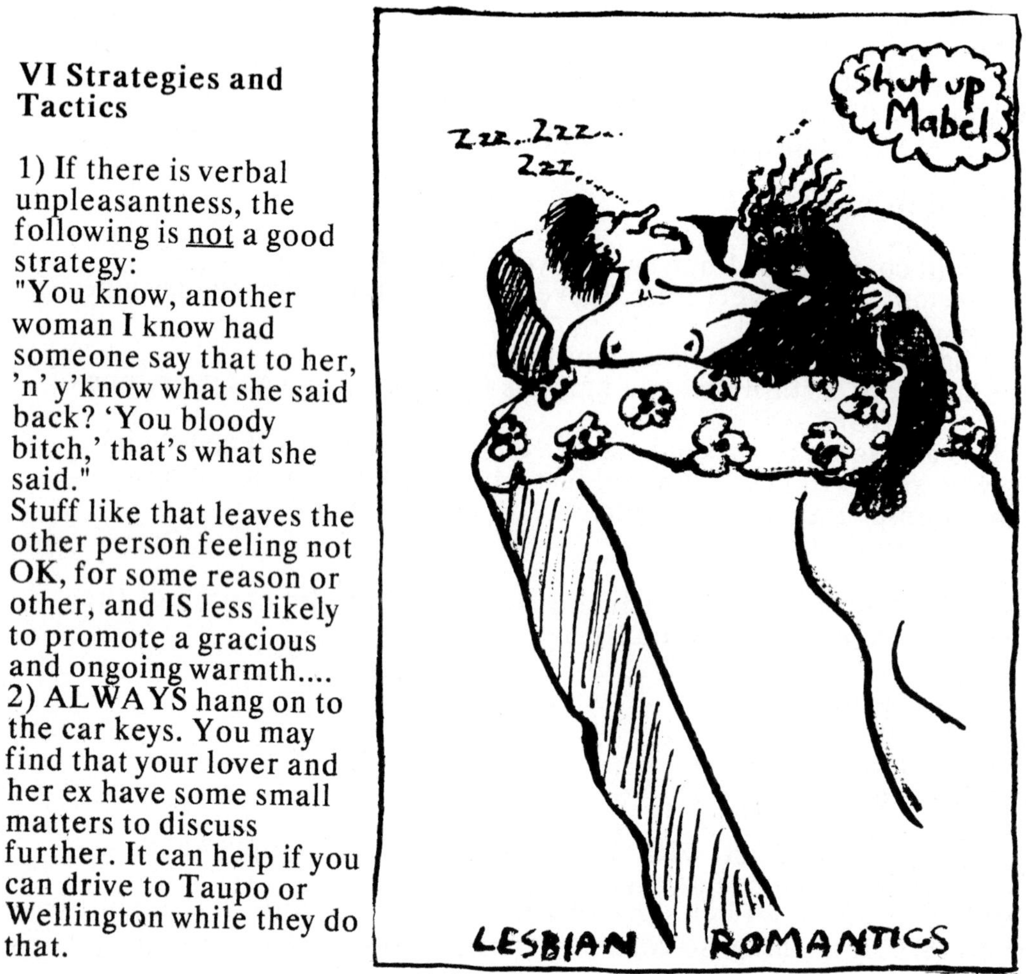

3) NEVER, if involved in a scenario where the ex lover is giving you a free character reading whilst standing over you with a bouquet of fives, yawn.
It is almost always misunderstood
4) Should by any remote chance, the ex show an intense desire to remodel your head against a brick fireplace, you should do the following:
State clearly that you are a pacifist, that you leave stuff like this to your lawyer, and pass out.
Do not even touch your assailant with the flick of your little finger.
If you do, she will burst into tears and tell everyone that you are a rotten bully. Worse yet, she will elicit tea, sympathy and Band-Aids from your lover - who knows where all these things are kept.

VII Things To Carry In Your Jacket Pocket:

Medic-Alert bracelet, twenty dollars just in case all your tyres are suddenly dead flat, - and the car keys, of course.
Face masks and Molotov cocktails are simply excessive.

****

The above document has been compiled after considerable field work.
However, because all ex's that have been in one way or another involved in my immediate circle are going to get paranoid about it, I've had to follow through with another booklet called "Total Rejection is O.K."
During my spell in hospital after publishing the above, I wrote a new study called "Total Rejection is O.K. Only If You are on the Winning Side."
Both books are available from PAPERTHEWALLANDOTHERCOVERS for only $24.95 and postage.
A meditation tape which includes low THUDDING SOUNDS, OCCASIONAL JEERS AND the occasional hysterical giggle combined with comments such as: "You've <u>who</u>?"
"You must be joking" or "What have you done with our duvet cover" is available on request.
It has been proved absolutely excellent for getting your karma together before Strange Encounters.

Juliet Bravo

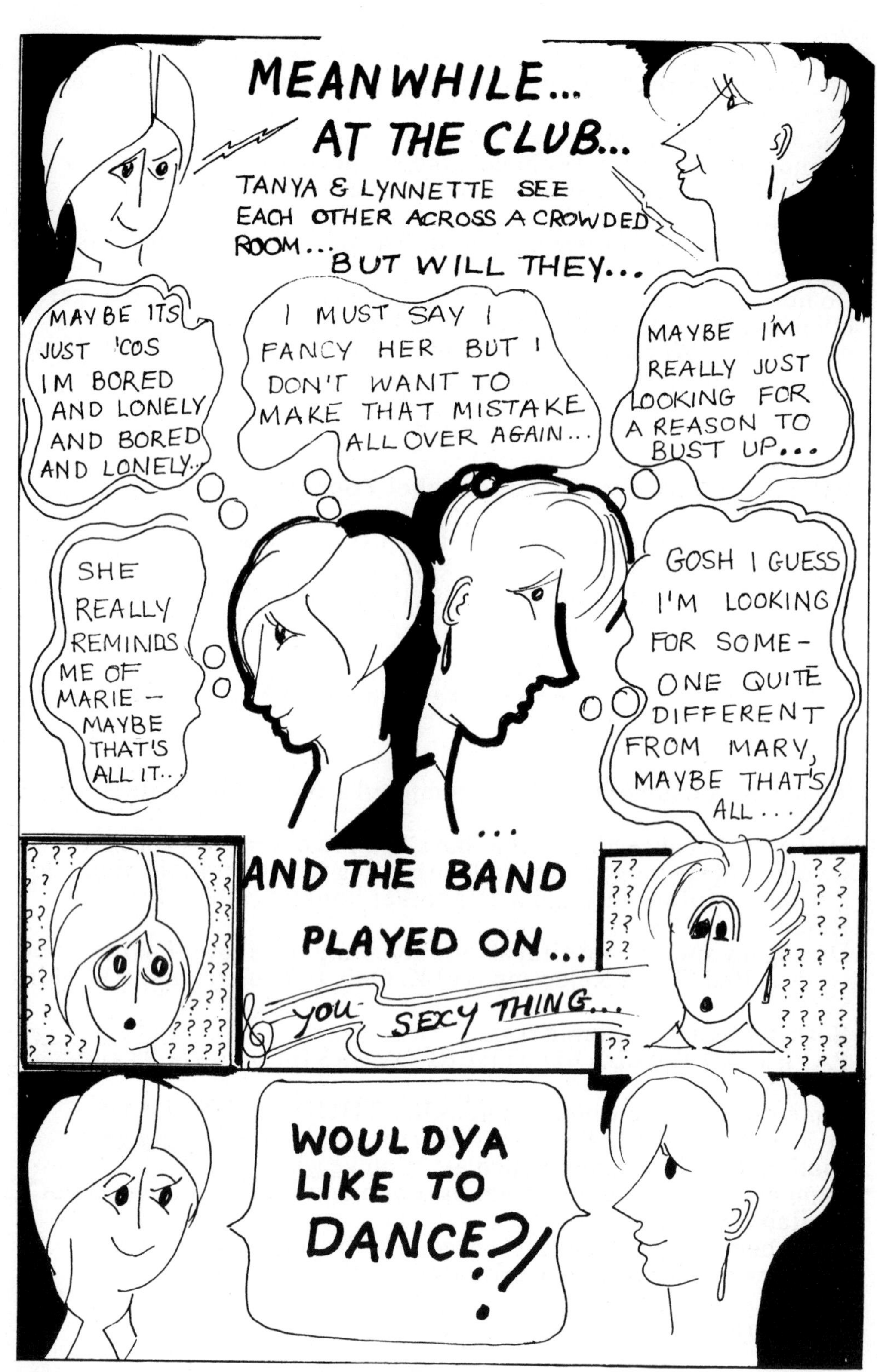
MEANWHILE... AT THE CLUB...
TANYA & LYNNETTE SEE EACH OTHER ACROSS A CROWDED ROOM... BUT WILL THEY...
MAYBE ITS JUST 'COS IM BORED AND LONELY AND BORED AND LONELY...
I MUST SAY I FANCY HER BUT I DON'T WANT TO MAKE THAT MISTAKE ALL OVER AGAIN...
MAYBE I'M REALLY JUST LOOKING FOR A REASON TO BUST UP...
SHE REALLY REMINDS ME OF MARIE – MAYBE THAT'S ALL IT...
GOSH I GUESS I'M LOOKING FOR SOME-ONE QUITE DIFFERENT FROM MARY, MAYBE THAT'S ALL...
... AND THE BAND PLAYED ON...
YOU SEXY THING...
WOULDYA LIKE TO DANCE?!

Mogs And Nogs

A. Nog

Enough of the talk of butch and femme. The real differences in our community are between mogs and nogs.

You'll be wanting some definitions (lesbians always like to split, or should I say part hairs). Here goes. A mog is a dyke who for some reason best known to herself prefers, or maintains that she prefers, monogamous relationships for herself and her lover. Nogs are the rest of us normal dykes, mostly held in thralldom to the rules that mogs try to set up.

Being a mog or being a nog is a basic personality difference which may have its origins in childhood. Mogs probably had sisters of the sort who lick all the cakes on the plate so that you can't eat any. Anyway, the sort of childhood where there wasn't enough to go around. To be more psychoanalytical, the development of object relations in mogs was such that they can entirely fixate on one love object at a time. Narrow, huh?
Maybe the difference is even genetic. Perhaps mogs have more focussed hormones.

Anyway, a mog and a nog together means trouble. The problem is, most relationships involve a mog and a nog. You hardly ever find two mogs together. The reason? Well, its obvious; they're essentially dull and don't excite each other. Two mogs together would be as flat as a failed souffle. They're more interested in nogs.

And why aren't nogs usually a number? Well, they try but, to put it kindly, there's little glue to hold them together. It's not long before they're off with someone else. The reason most couples are a mog/nog mixture is they are held together by a gripping conflict. Mogs like excitement (until they get it and find it's scary) and nogs like security (until they get it and find it's choking them).

In its stable, cosy moments, the mog-nog relationship seems to be going fine; and then when the nog starts finding life a little dull and looks elsewhere, the mog makes a fuss and the relationship becomes exciting again. So, the typical mog-nog relationship is two steps forward, three steps back and it can go on for years like this, with dull periods, exciting moments and a general slide down from the blissful beginnings.

The life of mogs and nogs together is punctured by long and meaningful discussions, irritable exchanges and downright quarrels about the superiority of moggishness or noggishness. Mogs tend to hold the morally superior ground. They read Naiad Press romances and they seize with excitement on any story they hear about two dykes who've lived together for 80 years. When they hear these stories, their eyes get soft and they tend to go "ohhhhhhhh", just like people do over photos of cute cats, cute kids and brides. They believe that in their romantic friendships, women of the 19th century were anaesthetized from the waist down.

Mogs are shocked and disappointed when couples they know split up and they disapprove of poaching. They love stories about triangles that didn't work and affairs that ruined relationships. They discuss trysts and other ways of getting married. They go to workshops on long-term relationships.They are often a wonderful shoulder to cry on for disappointed dykes in love. At their worst, they tend to say nasty things to their partner like: "Do you want to be lonely in your old age?"; and "Why are you so insecure that you have to try to destroy relationships?"

Mogs deny it if you tell them that they're repressed. And since they're wonderfully passionate in bed it's so blatantly untrue that it is hard to score with that argument. However, you can usually get to them if you tell them that they have such low self-esteem that they're too scared to risk coming on to someone else.

Nogs look back on the golden age of lesbian liberation when monogamy was supposedly disapproved of. (When was that and why wasn't I around?) They mutter about "It's only natural" and "Everyone fancies other people". To which mogs maddeningly reply, "Of course, but it's what you decide to do about it that counts".

Nogs spend much of their waking life thinking about the one or two or three women they currently fancy, wondering what they might do about it, trying to figure out how they can get into bed with them and not have a mess to deal with afterwards.

Occasionally they do, of course, and they do have a mess to deal with afterwards because unfortunately, mogs are very forgiving. I say unfortunately, because the expert mog immediately brings the focus of an extracurricular splurge right back on to the relationship. What's wrong with our relationship? is a theme that can drain energy endlessly. Or else they get so upset that the nog has to pay attention. And of course, if the errant one was foolish enough to fall into bed with another mog, she usually has quite a crisis going on there too.

In dealing with this mess, the nog finds it hard to get any public sympathy for having wreaked such havoc, though in one-to-one situations she will find many sympathizers (closet nogs).

A few bouts of this and the nog may fall into a permanent state of guilt-ridden self-pity. The worst outcome of this condition is that the next time she fancies someone she may decide to justify it by falling in love.

Some other differences. In their pitiable childhoods, mogs had fantasies of being foundlings. They always thought that they had been placed in the wrong family and that their father was really a prince and their mother was a woman with six breasts, a huge lap, a permanent apron and a desire to read stories continuously to them. Nogs, on the other hand, had orphan fantasies. They hoped everyone in their family would drop dead and then they would have an exciting life as a street urchin.

Another way of contrasting them is that mogs are eggs and nogs are apricots. Mogs often come across as warm, secure earth mothers. But do something harmless to them (like fall into bed with their best friend) and they tend to fall apart and show their soggy insides. Mogs can cry for weeks at a time, honest. That's why nogs often get arthritis in their left shoulder, from the constant damp. Nogs are apricots. They often seem neurotic, vulnerable and twitchy on the outside, showing all the symptoms of repressed sexuality. They tend to suffer from phobias, tics, irrational dislike of loud noises and occasional inability to get out of bed in the morning. Don't be fooled by this. Underneath this surface softness is a solid kernel, longing for adventure.

Nogs hate Naiad Press romances, though they love the detective novels where the PI falls into bed with her client on p.87. In the first six weeks of a relationship, they are capable of dewy-eyed fantasies about old age, but they soon start to find it irritating. They think that 19th century romantic friends definitely did it - all the time, behind their husband's backs. In fact, they tend to think that everyone does it all the time, except them. They're not good listeners to unhappy dyke tales, because unhappy dyke tales are nearly always about affairs, and envy gets in the way of the nog's listening ability.

Another way to tell a nog from a mog is that nogs are not huggy people. Mogs are very physically affectionate with lots of people (try to tell them that that's just how they get their kicks and you'll be told that you're childish and immature). Nogs feel awkward hugging other women because they are so busy thinking about what might happen next and trying to work out whether they want it to or what would happen if it did.

The most maddening thing you can say to a nog is "Well, how would you feel if you lover did it with someone else?" People always say this smugly, at the same time looking as if they've had an amazingly original thought and knocked you to the floor with an irrefutable argument. Nogs get jealous too. So what? To imagine how you feel about doing it with someone else should somehow be the same as how you feel about your partner doing it with someone else is the ultimate in idiocies and totally defies psychological reality. The person who says this to you is usually a mog herself. There is no suitable reply to this question, except pretending not to hear it.

The trouble with mogs is that they are basically dishonest. I mean, have you ever known a genuine fair dinkum mog? To qualify, you have to have had only one relationship in your whole life and it's still going.
Hands up, then. Do I see any hands waving? Mogs go on and on about "let's grow old together" with probably at least five different women over their life span. Mogs are doomed to serial moggery. Nogs, in my view, are the potential stayers, because they (try to) take time out to freshen up. They are not natural mergers.

In my ideal lesbian society, there would be lots of stable mog-nog couples. And there would be a secret society of nogs, with a secret handshake and password. They would rush off with each other from time to time and have dirty weekends (two at a time, I mean, just in case the grammar of that sentence is misleading). They would provide workshops occasionally to help those nogs who suffer from one of the worst disorders of lesbian psychology - compulsive honesty. And then we would all live happily ever after.

Editorial note:
A TIP FOR THE GUILTY: REMEMBER TO TELL HER IT WAS THE BEST YOU COULD DO AT THE TIME.

Q. How many mogs does it take to change a light bulb?
A. One, because her partner isn't home yet.

Q. How many nogs does it take to change a light bulb?
A. Two. One to change the light bulb and the other nog to be suggestive.
Or A hundred. One to change the light bulb and the others to provide ninety-nine possibilities.

Jealousy

Do I feel jealous you ask? Jealousy?!

Oh! I worked through that!

Yes! I now completely accept my lover's right to express her sexuality with whoever she chooses...

... she's a free individual ... a free spirit...

N RA
...and I love her very much.

... so why was I about to sprinkle RAT POISON on her cheese cracker?
RAT
Evachild

This Woman

This Woman
entices me with her presence,
her sun-heated skin suggests warmth.
Her dark-haired legs intrigue,
her sloped belly tempts,
her breasts cause great yearning,
her lips taunt with hued
softness. The body draws me;
a hand stretching,
finger flexing,
taste-bud squirting,
wish to touch.
This woman's eyes;
her eyes melt me,
flood me,
turning my lust,
hot tearing passion
to a deepened longing.

Lynn March

Coloured Candles

If you won't stay with
me I don't want to
spend another night
deciding whose place
we will sleep at.
I have spent a long
time making my bed,
the butterfly walls,
lavender drawings and
design. I have
matched the border at
the ceiling with the
carpet on the floor,
coloured candles with
perfumed pillows of
crisp embroidered
linen. Stars twinkle all
over Auckland but I
twinkle just here.

Miriam Saphira

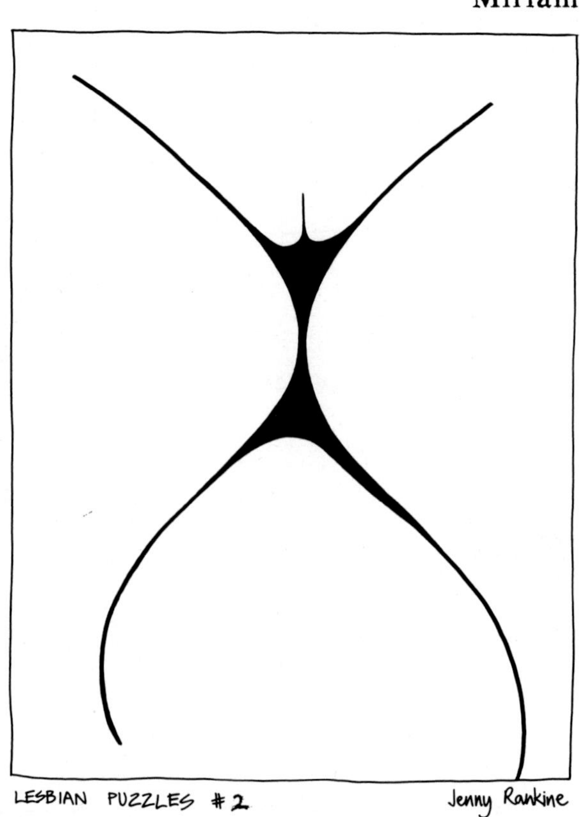

LESBIAN PUZZLES #2 Jenny Rankine

MADAM (MEIKLES HOTEL, ZIMBABWE, 1987)

A white woman
eating alone,
Slivers on a silver plate
grate on my teeth.
I wing in from a greasy backpacker
in King's Cross to this high rise quiet
chesnut opulence.
On the rooftop wellfed Rhodesians bake
-fat potatoes beside the pool.
Behind their sun-glasses,
they narrow their eyes at me
So obviously a fish out of water.

Swinging through the revolving doors,
I leave the pond behind.
Madam.
You'd better get used to it.
White woman.
Madam.

WHITE GIRLS (IN THE CLOSET)

Parasitic
You wind yourself around her neck.
The air is warm, fetid, going nowhere.
together you are an over-ripe fruit,
long since plucked.
Skin, but not flesh, absorbs my words.
Opening the door, the loud air hits me
fresh and strong.
I can't get out quick enough.

Kathleen

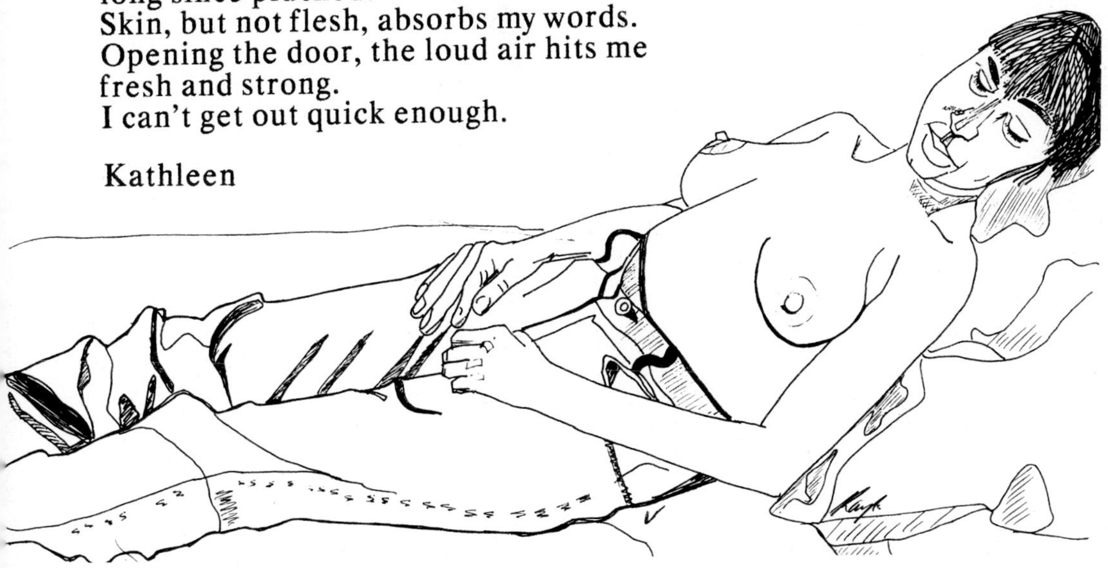

Teetering on The Borders of Love

From the western
horizon - like a
bicycle pedalling
interest in retrograde,
our bodies
encircle as we do
those celestial.
In one another's orbit
for such a short time
then gone, spinning
onward
until the return
which assured does
come,
again.

surface without depth
no guise
squander all intensity -
inebriate become unto
gain repute and raised
evident energy locked, latent,
turbulent
BUT: what, when, how, if,
and will?
fuck love

Ashlyn Ex

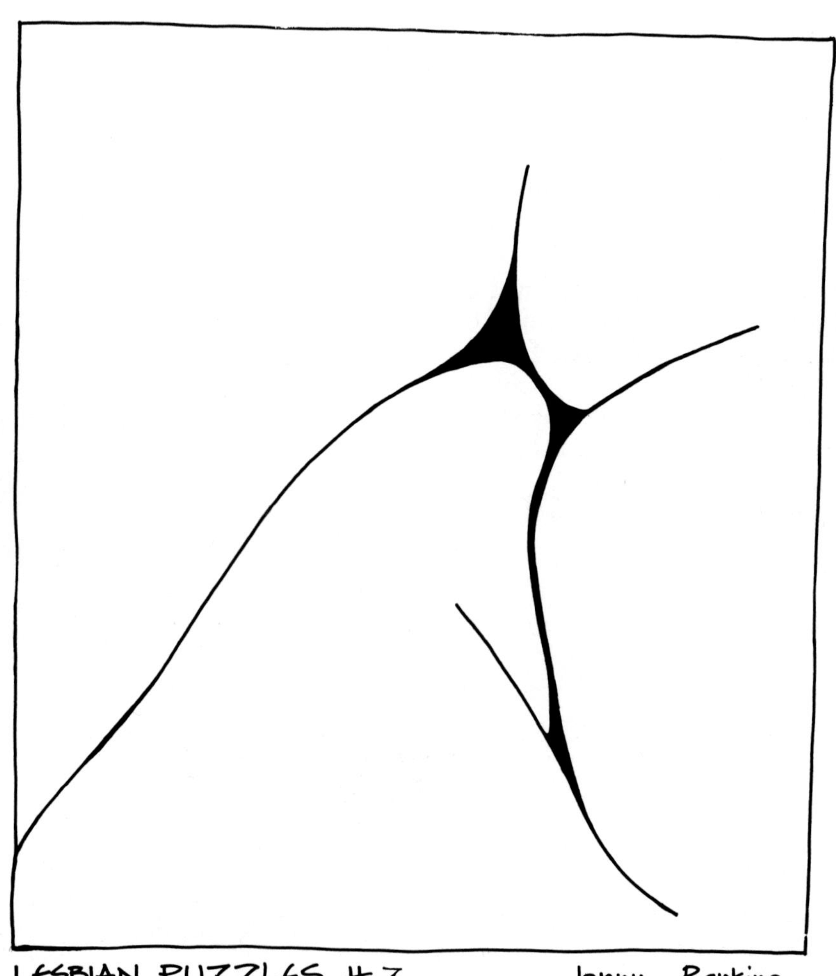

LESBIAN PUZZLES # 3 Jenny Rankine

Sarah

The coming of my anger
bursts
rejected on the ground
the frustration
of my love
mixed up
with gentle tenderness
to quick for me
to clutch
these arms that ache
to hold her
are severed by the mind
the line that runs
my bloods breathe,
breathe Sarah
and gathers in the
crutch of my desire
whenever she comes near.

I never asked to love her
impotent in my rage
against this nameless thing
that wills my feelings
how to grow
that horn of plenty
never blew her woman's love
to me
through all my days
  I've sought
for this
a woman's hand and
tender kiss
and deep and wise and gay
desired
and soft tongue
to fan the fire
and all my nights
  I've dreamed
  of Sarah

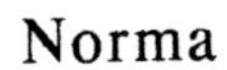

Norma

In Celebration Of Finding You

In celebration of finding you
I shared my idea;
you chewed, sucked them up
and hammered them to the bone.

In the joy of my discovery
I sang my sweetest song;
you looked away, snarled
and lisped hard words.

I found you again that night
curled, thin and white
mud-black eyes and
lips shaped like ltlle boats.
I took off your glasses
and held you.

You told
a woman's tale
of how they'd used you up.

Kaye Kemp

Warm Wind

I ride the warm wind
of honey-mist
above the pathways
and people.

I float untouchable
and will only descend
for you.

Kaye Kemp

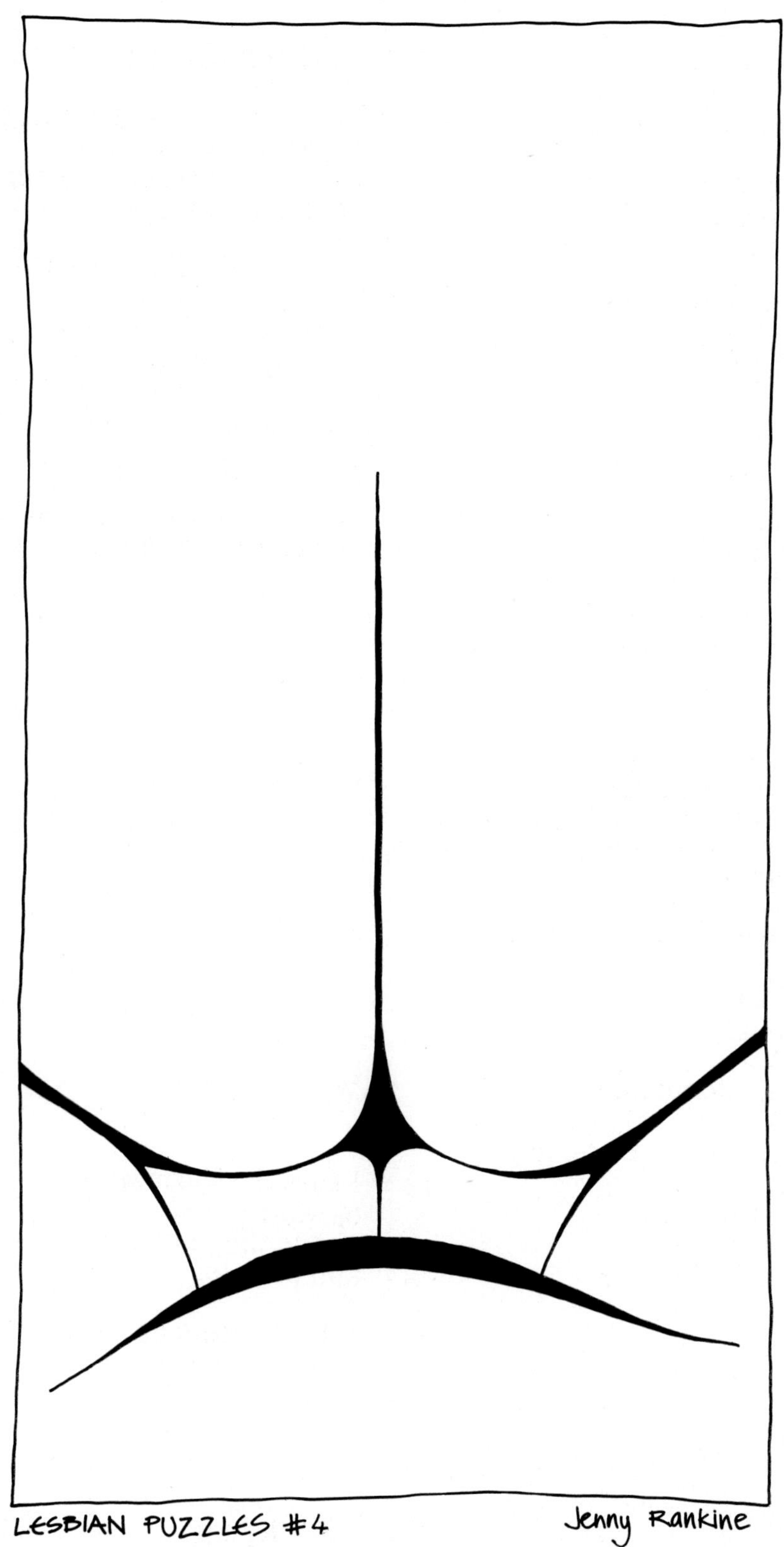

LESBIAN PUZZLES #4 Jenny Rankine

Home Cooking

Merrilyn wiped a couple of specks off the knife blade and carefully placed it on the linen table cloth. The air was full of cumin and coriander; she loved cooking; the fact that the house smelt like the back streets of Bombay delighted her. Warm sunlight fell across the vivid nasturtiums on the window ledge; outside bamboos clattered in the wind.

She opened a pleasant red wine and left it to snuffle away for a while. The kitten purred noisily; she absently stroked it, and stirred the chicken. Her tongue ran around the spatula thoughtfully. She ate a poppadom. Just checking. Perhaps if she changed the seating around, things would go better.

She would prefer to sit opposite Jan, but then she'd be too far away from the kitchen. And Jan would probably want to sit opposite Annie. Annie wouldn't want to sit next to Marion, though; they made such a point of not being a couple. Which was odd, because they did everything together. Marion was supposed to be the retiring one, the shy one, the one who didn't take the initiative. Jan said that, and Jan knew them better.
Funny, thought Merrilyn, could've fooled me. Annie always strikes me as being some kind of sweet pea caught in high wind. Merrilyn adjusted the nasturtiums, but thought about sweet peas. Little tendrils all over them that wind into chicken wire and other plants.
Rather be a nasturtium, she thought, bright and slightly vulgar and bitey.
The kitten jumped on the table. Merrilyn scooped it off, and went back to the rice.
Perhaps she could sit next to Jan and near the kitchen. No that was problematical... Perhaps they could have dinner in the lounge.

She tried to work out possible combinations and rearranged the table for buffet service.

The late sunlight was going to her head like dandelion wine. She felt the music getting to her. It was very slightly sentimental; National programme in the late afternoon .... and she looked over the lounge...

Two two-seaters and an armchair. I wonder what they'll do with this seating, she thought. Two of us and two of them, like Home Team and Away Team?

And Annie and Jan all set to win the match, whatever it was. Merrilyn felt suddenly that, dandelion wine, sunlight or no, a "quality control check" on the red wine was in order. The dry fullness warmed her mouth. Suppose they were dogs, she thought - Annie's the spaniel, all licky and rolling over, and Marion's more of a setter - those mournful brown eyes; "I can't eat -" - whatever food allergy she was currently into.... and Jan? Bit of an old fox terrier there, she thought - but me I'm an Airedale. Messy and intransigent.

The beginning of dinner was going to be a bit like that, she thought, everyone sniffing at everyone and deciding whether it would be war or peace ....

Perhaps it would be safer to imagine them as a Still Life With Fruits. More truthful, too.
There was a rising pungency from the kitchen area. Merrilyn opened the oven to this tropical blast of hot, spicy cuisine. Lovely.
Perhaps it would persuade Jan to stop ringing Annie, and vice versa. It was, she decided, a perfect domestic set piece, a theatrical statement of menage à deux. She was quite glad she had invited Annie and Marion, and she'd enjoyed the look of startled surprise as she had done so.
One day, she thought, I may well regret this being nice stuff. Perhaps I should put some poison in something..."Here's a nice cup of coffee for you, Annie...." and arsenic, you bitch. Or perhaps the big butch number and drag Jan off to the back of the cave, muttering territorial imperatives... She cast her horoscope backwards, thinking; I have been here before.
The door burst open. Jan, Annie and Marion pushed and cluttered their way in - the group, the team. There was a glossy brightness about them, fever. They clanked bottles of bubbly. Merrilyn stood at bay in her apron.
"Come on Merrilyn," yelled Annie, "We're going to a restaurant. Jan's shouting."

Jill Brame

LESBIAN INSOMNIA ... NOT ALL LESBIANS COUNT SHEEP!

ENDLESSLY REINVENTING...

Tracy. That's a good name. Audrey knew immediately what she looked like. Her hand moved by itself, briskly stroking out the lines of the face, then the body. Young and lithe. Cheerful. And innocent. A young woman discovering her sexuality. Audrey knew who Tracy was. Everyone had been Tracy once. That's what made her such a good character.

In the first panel, she drew her with her face in her palm, gazing dreamily out of the window, spreading a light grey wash for the pane of glass, just a few spots of paper left bare hinting at a face in the glass. Tracy's own face of course. Dreaming into herself but not seeing herself, imagining a lover.

Who would the lover be? Audrey drew the outlines of the second panel. Who is Ms Right? The traditional knight in shining armour? Why not? With a few quick strokes, Audrey filled the panel with window, a close up of the glass panes, four squares. Then a knight, a horse, the lilies of France on the pennant floating from the spear. Joan of Arc. Broken into four pieces by the panes of grey wash.
Boring, sighed Audrey inside her head, as she drew the third frame. A funny little play on heterosexual tradition, yes, and sometimes Audrey thought she was still stuck with it, which wasn't so funny. But Tracy would be more original than that.

Besides, Joan was a martyr, burnt at the stake for a witch. Women had had enough of martyrdom. Tracy was, or would be, a woman of the 21st century. Stroppy. Free. At ease in the world, expecting to master it. Not like Audrey had been, still was sometimes, despite her brave bright clothes, deliberately clashing, studiedly untidy. Despite her brave rebellious artist's lifestyle and her passion for women. Who is this unformed Tracy? Someone better and braver than Audrey, this 21st century woman.

Audrey drew her again, dropping the half formed story line, just brainstorming the images, letting them fall out of her pen. Tracy in space, floating in a big white and black shadowed NASA spacesuit. Except, of course, she couldn't show her face. A helmet's plate went black in space, protecting the wearer's face from a sunlight unrestricted by atmosphere. See out but not in. And that wouldn't work because everyone would assume her a him. Maybe in the 21st century it would be different. But Audrey was drawing Tracy for 20th century readers. Damn! She drew another frame.

Tracy on a balcony, leaning over, her elfin face and short hair out of synch with the Juliet gown. The Romeo in the garden looked awfully like Audrey, in odd eclectic clothes, motley but not Shakespearian. Audrey put the pen down, leaned her own face in her palm, and closed her eyes. The old brain just wasn't storming today. This wasn't original either. She squirmed. Old friend, Critic, was on overtime. She put her hands over her eyes and squinted into the darkness. Tracy .... She focussed. She concentrated. She crunched her eyes tight enough for stars to come out. Little blue and green firework displays shot off on the dark screen of her eyelids.

"Hello," Tracy said, stepping out of a white panel. "Looks like you're getting stuck. Let me have a go."
She picked up Audrey's pen and began sketching rapidly, talking all the while over her shoulder.
"You want me perfect. And in order to have me perfect, you have to perfect the world. It's too much. You're trying to tidy everything up like your underwear drawer. She shrugged, waving one hand.
You have to leave me incomplete. So I'll have something to invent myself. You know that really. You're a creative artist."

"I want you to be what I am not," protested Audrey, "what or who I never had a chance to be."
"Pooh," said Tracy. "You're making yourself all the time, reinventing the world. You'll never be finished, and you don't want to be either because growth doesn't stop. That's what's wrong with perfection; it leaves out everything really important."
"I didn't expect you to be so profound," Audrey said. "Thirteen is a bit young for all this philosophy. I'm only just finding out that sort of thing."

"The innocent are wise. Isn't that the cliche? Or if you like, I'm you, a part of you."
"But you're so cheerful, so hopeful. You're so much in love with yourself."
"I'm glad that you can see that," Tracy said, putting the pen down. "For a while, I thought you were getting lost in that Joan of Arc stuff."
"I hinted at it, in the first frame. You with your own face in the glass. The window as mirror."
"Everything is a mirror. Other people. Things."
"The people I make up," suggested Audrey.
"Exactly."
"Are you saying I'm in love with myself?"
"I'm hoping you'll discover that you're worth being in love with."
"That sounds so vain."
"Patriarchy says that. Remember to reverse the patriarchial mode to find the truth."

"Mary Daly," grumbled Audrey. "I never liked her." She opened her eyes, and Tracy whisked back into the last frame, the one she had drawn herself. Or the one Audrey had drawn with her eyes closed. Tracy was dreaming into the window just like the first frame. Only it was Audrey, disorganized, rebellious Audrey she was gazing at.
It wouldn't do for a LIP cartoon, but Audrey pinned it on her wall anyway. You never knew what was going to come out when you put pen to paper.

Nancy Peterson

ACT I

How it ever began she really couldn't explain, not to herself let alone anyone else.
It was a strange unsettling time for her, beginnings and endings all mixed up and no real way of telling whether babies were being thrown out with their bathwater or whether in fact new brooms were about to sweep squeaky clean.

There she was knowing that she was at the end of her marriage but unable to move on. Stuck, coming unstuck.
She had begun to dream of women, lovely women, loving women, intimate women relating, women lovers. These women were becoming more and more intrusive, walking in and out of her rather desperate reality in a way that defied efforts to concentrate on being a sensible responsible middle-aged wife and mother.
So when the young woman of the crisp dark curls and eyes of unbelievable promise appeared the ground had been well and truly prepared for sproutings of unbelievable proportions.
Not that it happened quite like that. No heart lost at first glance scenario. She was the daughter of a colleague, not long out of school and no more important than the children of colleagues ever are. Sometimes they distinguish themselves, usually as nuisance value and less often as interesting people-to-be all potential and no past, puppy fat and unformed minds. Very unlikely love material.
So how did they begin those glances, meaningful from lustrous eyes; those moments of suspended breath; awareness of the other's presence, close but not touching; exchanges of confidences; seeking of time to spend together?
Until the day came when she knew that something had to be said, some spell untangled/broken, some honest word spoken. And having no words to say she put her arms around the girl and there was a moment when a drawing back was still possible because of...
"I'm frightened of you" and a drawing back.
"Oh, oh well" she said with resignation. What was it she wanted anyway?
But the young one knew what she wanted and began the kisses that led to more, sitting on the floor, drowning in them. Walking to the sea, lying on the stony beach aware of nothing but the other and the kisses.

And later, on the bed back at the house during the longest afternoon ever, the touching, the whispered,
"Do what you want with me, you know it's what I want."
Panic. What do you want me to do with you? And what do I want you to do with me? A decade of marriage and numbers of boyfriends before that had not prepared her for this. It was mostly clumsy fondlings that afternoon, nothing like she later came to know as

lesbian sex. The soul-encompassing mirroring of each other, sensual and spiritual combined.
However, for all its awkwardness, that afternoon cata-pulted her out of somnambulance into sharp awareness of how badly she misfitted her situation. Everything from then on sped up. The next year had a nightmarish quality. Act one begun.

Rhona

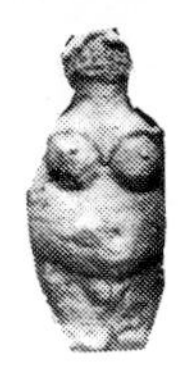

Home Sweet Lavender Home

Womb With A View

Life begins in the round; the very basis of life being a cell.
The first months of our lives are spent within the curvature of our mother's womb where we are nurtured and await the time of our entry into this world. When we do enter, it is through the velvet cave and the curling gateway of the vagina.
Is it any wonder then that many women reflect in the immediate, outer world of their homes, the rounded, nurturing space of that inner world of their bodies.
Have you ever considered the images in the homes that you feel comfortable in? Maybe you are familiar with the arching of light through crystals. Perhaps you remember images of bowls, bottles and jars both slender and voluptuous. You may have noticed the placement of furniture to soften the angles of corners, the caress of the cushions, the pebbles and shells that invite your touch, the plants that spill their curves upon walls and shelves. There may have been images of women and woman shapes in paintings and print, carved from wood and stone erupting in glass.
Next time you are sitting comfortably you may wish to cast your senses wide and take a look around.

On the following pages there are some of these ideas in our interior design feature. The photos were taken in lesbian homes in and around Auckland.

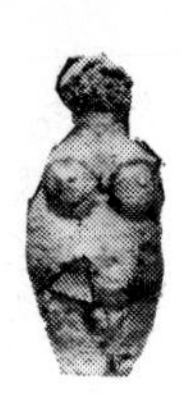

ARE SPIDERS PECULIAR ?

Is Blackie peculiar? She lives beside our bath and leaps out at the patter of tiny fly feet, or any other quiet noise. Her home is a minute crack in the wood, hardly an opening really, scarcely big enough for such an enormous spider to rush from, but suddenly, she's there, right beside me. I've never seen her catch anything but she watches me a lot, lolling in the bath. At first I found this unnerving and couldn't look at her watching me. But after all she is a woman spider. That first time, the atmosphere was a bit tense. I had to persuade myself I was too big for her to catch, really, eh. And drag back to her lair. Now I've grown fond of her. She's almost one of the family. I expect her to appear when I rustle around in the bath - and if she doesn't I feel quite rejected.

Annabel Fagan

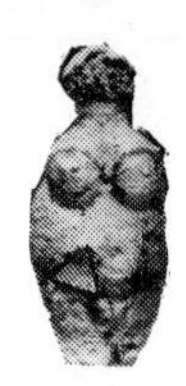

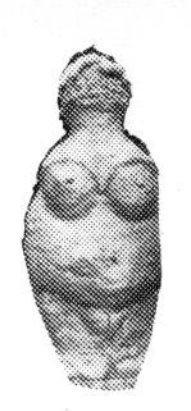

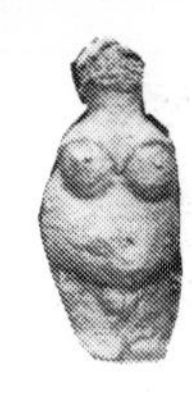

Environmental Design 200 Years Ago

In Exmouth there is a five storey hexadecagonal house which has been handed down the female line ever since it was built by two women in 1794.
Miss Jane Parminter and her younger cousin Miss Mary built A La Ronde, as it is called, in such a way that the viewer is deceived by the perspective. For instance, if you stand in the middle of the hall the height of the cupola appears to be 100 feet high but is actually only 35 feet.
There are eight rooms going off the central hall but each room has a door to the next so that it is possible to move from room to room without going into the tall hallway which would have been difficult to heat in the winter. Although the house is quite eccentric it is a practical house with the rooms following the sun, with the morning room in the east to the oval drawing room windows looking out at the sunsets in the west. The octagonal hallway and the eight rooms form eight wedges with the hexadecagonal outside wall. These wedges were made into storage spaces for each room. To save space the doors between the rooms actually slide into the walls - something that was not typical of the 18th century. The central hall was used for dancing and when you were sitting out a turn you could use the small foldaway seats which pull down across those eight doorways. When not in use the seats look like a carved wall panel. Much of the interior design is influenced by the women's travels, particularly in Italy. However, the most astonishing features inside are the arrangements of feathers and shells into patterns for they are so similar to certain arrangements in lesbian houses in 1989 Ponsonby. In making the feather dado and cornice each feather was placed in such a way that it

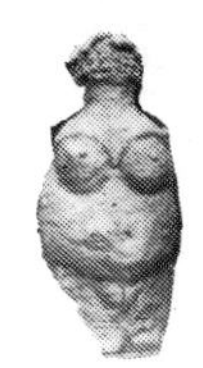

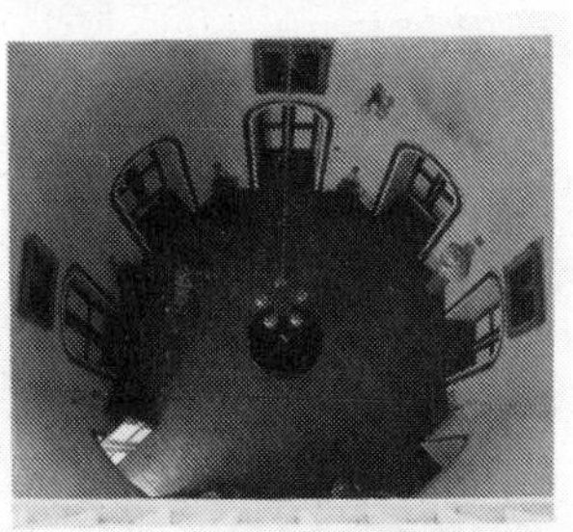

would not attract dust. There is also the grotto gallery which is completely decorated with shells, cowries, mussel and cockle shells which have been graded according to shape, colour and size. Every now and then there is a witty addition of a thimble or a tiny piece of porcelain.

Miss Jane and Miss Mary settled in Exmouth and built A La Ronde after travelling through Europe with two other female companions for ten years. They set off when Miss Mary was 17 years old and recently orphaned and Miss Jane was 34 years old. Their concern for single women and orphans is apparent from the small residence they built in the grounds to accommodate six orphan girls from the parish. It is placed near the small chapel which they also built. Their woman's orientation is so clear in the details they considered. Atop the steeple instead of a weathercock they placed a weatherhen.

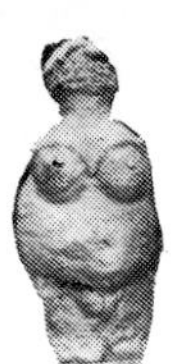

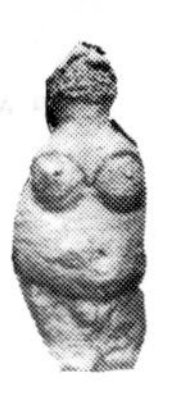

THE LESBIAN SPA

THE ECONOMY MODEL

Kathleen Rose

"You know you shouldn't be smoking in here, Kathleen. Really!"
Kathleen Rose looked up into the aide's frowning face.
"If matron catches you we'll all be for it!"
Kathleen Rose studied the aide's cross expression.
'Look - you've got ash all over the quilt.'
Kathleen Rose watched as the aide's hands brushed at the ash, marking it grayly across the cover.
"It's so dangerous, and it's bad for your health. I bet your lungs look like the inside of a coal mine!"
Kathleen Rose had once been down a coal mine and hadn't minded it a bit. .
"It's n(vonder you cough in the mornings."
Kathleen Rose didn't but she obliged now with a short dry cough.
"And I'll bet you've been using the hand basin for an ash tray." The aide tucked the sheets firmly under the mattress. Kathleen Rose hated the sheets tucked in. "If you insist on smoking then you must do it out on the verandah."
Kathleen Rose moved over to the small hand basin beside her bed and under the guise of washing her hands flushed the cigarette butt down the plug hole.
"There - that's better." The aide stood back from the bed. "All done, neat and tidy. Now," she turned to face Kathleen Rose, "remember what I said - out on the verandah."
"... remember what I said, remember what I said," Kathleen Rose mouthed as the aide hurried from the room. Why did they have to go on - worrying about her lungs, her health. Shoot, she was seventy-nine years old, with nothing to live for, and they were worrying about her health! Not that there had been too much wrong with it before she entered The Haven! A bit of cramp and the usual twinges, but nothing she couldn't live with. She could still walk to the shops, do her garden and her own housework ...

It was that strange disorientating bout of forgetfulness that had landed her in trouble; the day she walked out of the drapery shop with a singlet still clutched in her hand! And what a fuss they had kicked up! - Yes, of course they had known her for years, and yes, of course they knew she was honest, but still.... But still they had phoned the local police, and everyone had seen when he came to the shop to talk to her, and everyone, later, knew about it. In a small town gossip could travel faster than fire. And worse, she couldn't even remember picking the dratted thing up!

The humiliation lingered long, preyed on her mind, worried her to the extent that she became forgetful around her own home; leaving taps turned on, windows wide open at night and, finally, leaving the hot plate on full heat. When the firemen had finished their rescue operation there wasn't much left of her kitchen except wet-smelling blackened walls and a slush of charred debris covering the floor.

Kathleen Rose knew that Church's were supposed to be there to save people's souls from sin, but never having considered herself to be any sort of sinner she had kept away from them. After the fire the local

church welfare, backed up by the local doctor, suggested she would be better to move further into the community, where her little absences of memory could be contained in the embrace of a caring and nurturing environment. Living on her own, so far from help, could be a worry for them all,and it was, after all, her welfare they had in mind. Wouldn't she rather have peace of mind?

Kathleen Rose thought she would have peace of mind if they left her alone to get on with her own things. But, they questioned, how would she repair the house? She had, after all, only her pension. Yes, that was a problem, but perhaps being such caring and concerned persons as they were, they would help her out there? Well, really, they were geared to 'housing' people not repairing houses, and they had perfectly adequate accommodation, in the city, for someone like Kathleen Rose; on her own in the world, with material encumbrances like house repairs, maintenance, ill-health. Much better that she hand it all over to them - let them deal with it, lift the whole load from her mind ...

There was a time when Kathleen Rose had not been alone in the world.. there had been Agnes. But Agnes was long gone. Too young, too early, too soon. Ah, those twenty years, when she and Agnes had each other. There was never another Agnes. Sometimes, in memory, those twenty years seemed like yesterday. So close, so much around her still.

So, finally, worn down by a combination of self doubt and others persuasion, Kathleen Rose allowed her house to be sold, allowed her body to be moved into The Haven, somewhere in the outskirts of the city. Found herself in the lonely confines of a small bedroom in a large house of many rooms and many strangers. Allowed herself six cigarettes a day from the pittance of personal money handed into her keeping each month, and allowed herself to wonder just how it had all happened and what she was doing there.

Her lapses of memory never bothered her again. At times she almost wished they would. To know where, why or how might be a blessing. There were others in The Haven who lived out their total existence oblivious of the reality around them. Kathleen Rose, head down (as had become more her habit lately) would study them, surreptitiously, wondering if they were better off with or without perception. There was no way of knowing but, she thought, kindly or unkindly, they were, in their present environment, probably better off without.

Kathleen Rose longed for the soft fresh feel of the grass under her bare feet. To stand in the open, clear air, of the night, giddy from viewing the vast panorama of stars and moon and wondering where it all began and if it ever ended. To pick sprigs of wild-growing bergamot and smell it's wondrous lavender scent as she pressed the leaves against her bare flesh behind the top of her frock. To see awesome early morning sunrises, or to walk freely and feel the rain on her skin.

Kathleen Rose yearned to go home, but she no longer knew, for sure where home was.
Not for her sitting around talking about husband, or children, or grandchildren ...

Kathleen Rose, with outright defiance, sat on the edge of her newly made bed and reached for her cigarettes. Two down, four to go - but what the heck! - maybe she would smoke seven today - even eight, if she felt like it!
She looked out of the window, her eyes following the flight of a lone sparrow. "Hullo, sparrow," she said, through the thin trail of smoke curling up from her fingers and past her face, "let me introduce myself, should you ever pass this way again - I am Kathleen Rose."

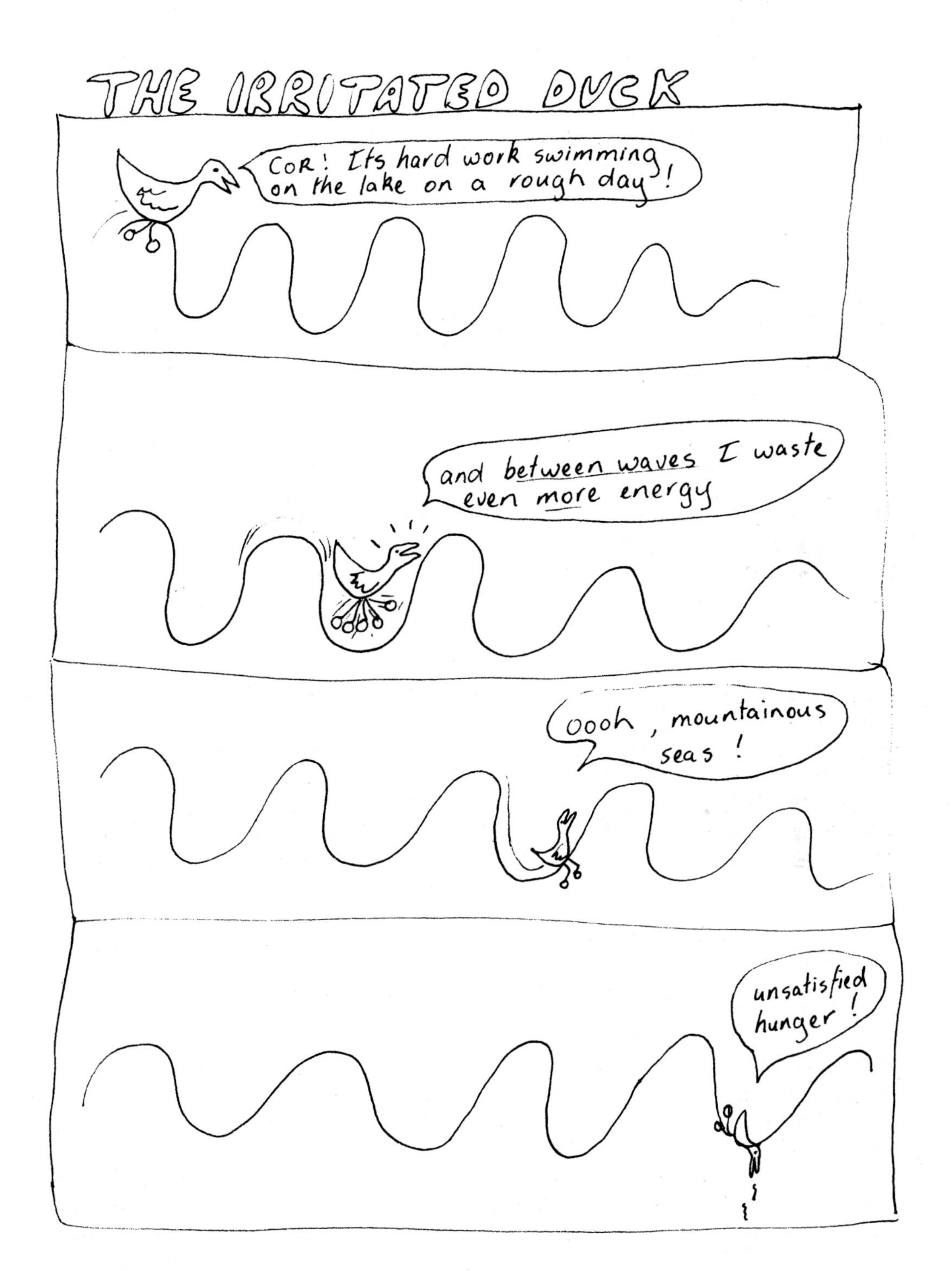
THE IRRITATED DUCK
COR! Its hard work swimming on the lake on a rough day!
and between waves I waste even more energy
oooh, mountainous seas!
unsatisfied hunger!

QUACK! Are those distant figures ashore distributing bread to the needy?
speed on fair duck!
hnfff!!
All this for a morsel of bread
mmm. Its a bunch of women. Might have guessed – the charitable sex.... aren't they lovely?

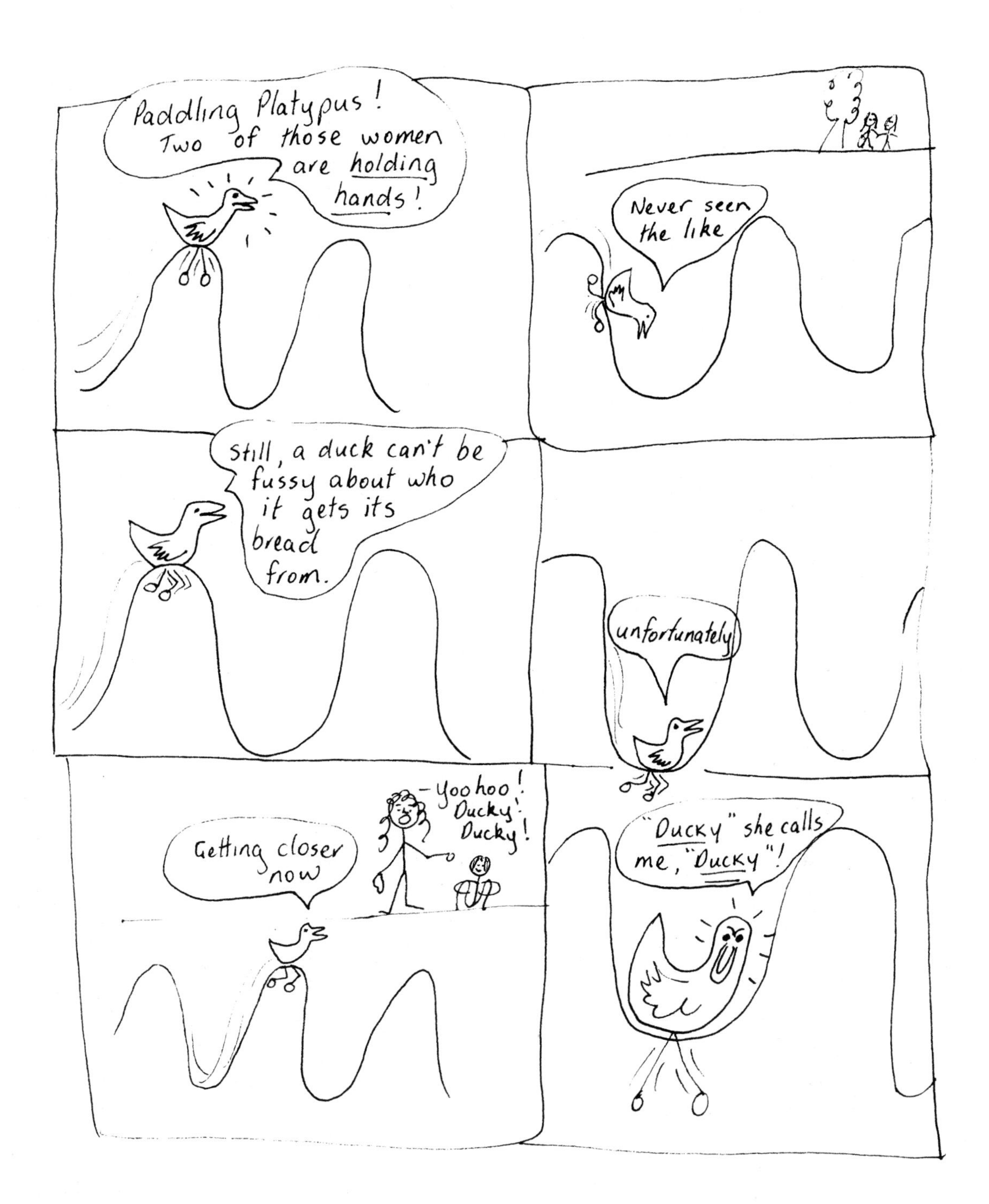
Paddling Platypus! Two of those women are holding hands!
Never seen the like
Still, a duck can't be fussy about who it gets its bread from.
unfortunately
Getting closer now
-Yoohoo! Ducky! Ducky!
"Ducky" she calls me, "Ducky"!

Oh the degradation a self respecting duck must suffer just to fulfil its basic needs!

Oh well. It will all be worth it to get my beak around some of that soft white yielding substance... BREAD!

yummmm!

Blarch! Quark!

I MIGHT HAVE KNOWN with these bloody lesbian feminists — WHOLEMEAL!

How lesbian are you?

For those of us who like to read about lesbians or women who loved women from earlier times we are frequently asked how we know that a particular person loved another woman. After all, close passionate friendships were fashionable at various times throughout history. Lillian Falderman's work in *Surpassing the Love of Men* has many excellent examples of these relationships.[1] The usual question is did she do it? This places an emphasis on lesbian sex and, while for modern lesbians getting it off is obviously quite important (see Joanne Loulan's work, *Lesbian Sex, Lesbians Passion,* and Emily Sisily's *The Joy Of Lesbian Sex*)[2,3,4] but just how important is sex between women in our lesbian relationships. Or for that matter, how important is sex with men in defining our lesbianism? In a very thought provoking article *Lesbian Sex -Is It?* Linda Strega and Bev Jo do not define anyone who welcomes semen into her body as a lesbian[5]. In their definition if a woman has ever had sex with men she has become a bisexual.

How did we know?
There are many different experiences of discovering ourselves but this excerpt will probably contain some of the componants of our coming out.

"I remember my first awareness of sexual feelings when I was 11 years old. The source of these feelings was another girl my same age at Campfire Girls... I could hardly keep my hands off her. I thought she was magic. I was that naive and we were incredibly happy. ...It was not until I had gone on to junior high that the full realisation of what those feelings meant to other people came crashing down on me. It was at that time I heard the words "queer" and "homo" for the first time, and I felt very ashamed and guilty".[6]

What is a lesbian orientation?
Lesbian orientation can be seen in eight broad factors. These are sexual behaviour, sexual attraction, erotic fantasies, body language, emotional preference, cultural preference (including dress code, environmental design, and social lifestyle) labelling and political attitude.
These factors can be most usefully seen on a continuum of heterosexuality, bisexuality, and homosexuality (figl).

The importance of each factor will vary among us according to our own understanding and experience. This will change over time and in different situations.

This continuum can also be broadened to include a wide range of attraction than a two sex (male and female) dichotomy. After all I

Figure I

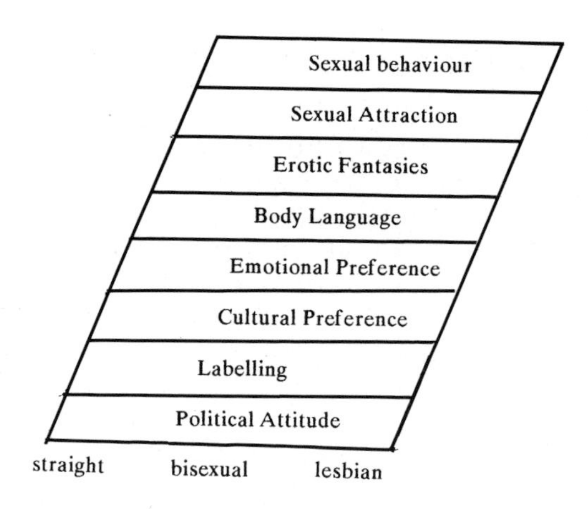

might be attracted to only butch women or femme women or androgenous individuals so the continuum can be widened as in fig II.

Figure II

masculine lesbian............................ masculine straight
androgenous lesbian .... androgenous straight
feminine lesbian .... feminine straight

Sexual attraction

Sexual attraction has been defined in terms of attraction to other sex, same sex and both sexes.[7] It does not include categories other than male and female. If someone's orientation includes fetishes there is no classification given for these. One can presumably classify leather, shoes and underwear as either male or female but what of an attraction to transexuals, drag queens or androgenous persons? Some writers classify all these as other than straight usually homosexual.[8]

Even defining the word "sexual" poses problems. A personal or social context is usually used to depict an attraction or behaviour as sexual.[9] Admiring an earlobe or nape of the neck may be sexual to one person and not to another, at one time and not at another, and in one setting and not in another.

So who or what do you fancy?

Sexual Behaviour

Sexual behaviour appears to be more easily defined if it is limited to sexual activity with a person. If a woman has not had any sexual activity it is clear that she can still have a sexual orientation but the labelling will probably be either heterosexual or, other than heterosexual. Some historians defining lesbian chose the Blanche Wiesen Cook's definition, "Women who love women, who choose women to nurture and support, and to create a living environment in which to work creatively and independently, are lesbians." However, while sexual behaviour may be absent for some lesbians, for others, such as male-identified lesbians it can be the only defining characteristic. As Francis Doughty states, "I keep coming back to the issue of sexuality: it is important to me why some...women loved each other physically and others did not express their love in full sexuality.

These same characteristics appear in studies of married gays. [11] [10]

It is difficult to ascertain how much lesbian sex warrants a label of lesbian. Talking about gay men Crowley puts it in the play, "The Boys In The Band": [12]

"One time it's youth. Twice, a phase maybe. Several times you like it." Whether a woman says they have changed their orientation or, had a lesbian relationship despite being heterosexual depends on the politics of disclosure rather than on having an articulated conscious theory of sexual orientation.

So who are you having it off with?

Sexual Fantasies

Fantasies used during masturbation were seen by Anna Freud as the criterion for ascertaining a person's sexual preference.[13] Classical Freudian theory would predict that unsatisfied needs lead to primary process thought concerning relevant objects. Behavioural theory would predict that using a particular fantasy over a period of time would condition the sexual response in that direction.

In a sample of married women with bisexual experience it was found that their fantasies included few females until after the bisexual experience.[14] Then female fantasies increased considerably. There is some evidence that straights report more heterosexual fantasies than lesbian fantasies and lesbians report more lesbian fantasies than heterosexual fantasies.[15]

Not all sexual fantasies are based on people. Humiliation and sado-masochism images may not involve sex typed individuals. Fantasies involving sensual experiences to oneself, autoerotic, could be construed as same sex fantasies. We often have a wide range of fantasies and it might be fun to make a sliding scale.

Body Language

Part of the sexual self can be the very sensual nature of one's self. One of the features of a closeted lesbian population, particularly in countries where lesbianism behaviour is illegal, is the ability for lesbians to seek each other out. They do this by reading the body language of others as an indicator of sexual orientation. A high degree of accuracy is needed as a mistake can mean a lengthy prison sentence or death. These clues can be the way the person stands, the eye contact, body posture in relation to either sex, and intonation.

Emotional Preference.

Fritz Klein uses the word "emotionally close to" but the expression "fall in love with" may be more descriptive.[7] Historically it has not always been possible to assume the sexual expression of an intimate emotional relationship and there may be sexual activity with no desire for emotional involvement at all. An emotional preference may refer to the person with whom you have a primary relationship or the person with whom you are having an affair, (that is, not living together).

For some people it is their emotional involvement that leads them to form a lesbian identity.

"One day when we were in bed, Sue my lover, asked me, 'Are you a lesbian, or do you just love me?' I really couldn't answer but I began looking at women everywhere, the shops, on the streets, at the beaches. I would watch their movements and wonder about that - Am I really? Am I?" [15]

Cultural Preference and Lifestyle

The lifestyles of lesbians have some commonality through class and ethnic similarities and differences but they also have their own characteristics.

A lesbian lifestyle could be made up of cultural preferences, dress code, role preference, environmental design and socialisation. Within factors there are a range of characteristics that suggest sexual inclinations. The handkerchief patterns of lesbians with a sado-masochism inclination is an example.

The amount of conformity to a lesbian dress code, environmental design and culture would seem to have a close relationship with the extent of the person's lesbian identity. These may add to a sense of belonging to the lesbian community and can offset a lack of, or reinforce, sexual behaviour and liaisons.

Social preference has been suggested as a significant factor in sexual orientation.[7] However, both straight and gay women may socialise almost exclusively with the same sex without giving us a clear indication of their sexual orientation. Closeted gay men may find they have to restrict their socialisation with women because it will be assumed that if they are not trying to have sex with the women they must be gay. This is due to the heterosexist assumptions of western society.

While many lesbians choose to socialise with other lesbians they may also socialise with heterosexuals owing to a wide range of common interests. Lesbians living in small communities may have no other lesbians to socialise with. Closeted lesbians would find their camouflage threatened should they socialise with other lesbians.

Political Attitude
There is some interrelationship between lifestyle factors, self-identification and political attitudes. However, political identification may be the only lesbian aspect of a person's sexual orientation. While this may be common in lesbian feminist communities it is almost non-existent among gay men as a basis for their self-identification. [17]

Radicalesbians maintain that heterosexuality is a political construction, a compulsory institution into which women are coerced and which is no more natural than high rise flats and the neutron bomb.[18]
A political attitude of lesbianism can be seen as a threat to the liberal humanist attempts to co-opt lesbians under the patriarchial power structure and calling ourselves lesbian can be an intregal part of this factor.

Labelling or Self-identification
Calling yourself a lesbian may be the most salient aspect of our sexual orientation but it is not a necessarily essential in the perception by someone else. Older lesbians may prefer to call themselves camp, gay, AD/DC, and different. Doctors frequently call lesbian mothers 'bisexual' just because they have had sex with a man at some time. But a woman who has had sex once or twice with women is never called a 'lesbian' by those in power unless it can be used in a derogatory way to put her down.

So for all this the main frame is "I am what I am".

A Cultural Feast

This year proved to be a cultural feast for lesbians down under. There has been a great array of talent across the country. We had the Gypsy Caravan Tour around Aotearoa (New Zealand) by the ***Topp Twins***, singing all our favourite songs. It even brought the lesbian truckers to town for the shows. The truckers live and work from their caravans and trucks as they move around the country, which makes some of the city dykes envious of their freedom.

Then we had the play of the decade, ***Frontwomen***. What a treat! Even the straights were enthralled by it. Congratulations to author Lorae Parry and we hear it might be made into a movie so here's hoping. ***Frontwomen*** is about a public figure who is lesbian, who falls in love with a married woman who leaves the straight world for love. Most of us have left something, work, family, school, drink and so on for love. The play excels in its ordinariness and I loved the way all the family open the fridge door as soon as they arrive home.

We didn't get much lesbian content on the telly this year apart from the sporting fixtures but we can hope for better things soon or at least a rerun of ***The Marching Girls***. We had a sucessful conference in Christchurch, several burgeoning youth groups established and a delightful festival in Hamilton. Here the Theatre Sports were heralded as the funniest show since ***Born To Clean*** by Renee. Whoever heard of a nation where there are no couples and everyone is in a menage a trois! and a nation which is 90 percent lesbian and the hets are in the closet! Some of Theatre Sports have been captured on video so we look forward to seeing it around the country for everyone to enjoy.

Another video we hope to show soon in the South Pacific is the wonderful lesbian soap, ***Two In Twenty Cos One In Ten Sounds Lonely*** which I was so lucky to have the opportunity to see when I attended the 1988 London Lesbian Summer School. It was such a shot in the arm for lesbian pride to have a lesbian soap.

We look forward to seeing what 1990 will bring but from the talent around it looks like it will be a lesbian cultural feast.

The Marching Girls

The Marching Girls is a TVNZ series of seven episodes which were screened in October 1987. Marching as a sport seems to be something peculiar to New Zealand and America and the series looked at the lives and in some cases the loves of the team memebers. The episode that struck a chord with the lesbian community was *Kerry's Story,* where Kerry, a busdriver and part-time band drummer falls in love with a passenger, a woman. Unfortunately the passenger turns out to be straight. Sounds familiar, but so great to see on our screens. Thank you Fiona Samuels and Melanie Read for that episode.

Talking Positions

Choose a Setting

say, the 13th floor, a penthouse with three walls half-glassed, uncurtained and surrounded by high rise buildings, waiters, shadow presences, under which we

Draw the characters

three watchers on settee, couch and humpty, come to watch The Marching Girls and afterwards go dance at Mariana's, swap our movements: love work remembering friends... projects ills discoveries shifts trends - make that, as always, we talk politics, survival

Ad-lib the last catch-up among close women

while black on a blue night sky the buildings splay, a loosening rakau bouquet, a child's black brush-stroke flat-painted overseers and parents ... though some obsessive draughtsman has filled their innards in, made a palisade of hollow honeycomb uprights; one, tall and thin as a lift shaft, ascetic preacher of a fanatic breed, bares in its lit-up cells a distant purgatory, in which small figures walk bent across the screens, turn and walk back, still bent, double over and disappear, emerge in another screen pushing handles, lifting buckets, stretching, scrubbing, rubbing, dusting, stage-hands in a curtain-raiser set up for the matinee

Who is it sings the untouchables

- Smoked mussel, anyone?
- Mmmm. Mmm.
- What's in them?
- Capers...peppers ...
- ... and something sweet
- garlic. In the marinade.
- Mussels are very - organic, aren't they.
- Definitely female. What are you discarding?
- I don't eat tongues. Or feet.
- But you don't turn down the lips?
- Ha.
- You couldn't eat too many though. Not like pulled off the rocks and steamed in a smidgin of sea water... these are a richer breed.
- Not so indigestible as some other seasoned luxuries...
- It's cost not taste curtails my appetitie.
- Contamination curbs mine. Our rocks stew in the sewage outlet.
- Wine, anybody?
- I suspect like other endangered species these are farmed.
- Definitely female. Anyone got the time?
- Time for - da-dum - The Marching Girls. Now, how many of us ...?

RECOUNT YOUR PRESENCES. YOUR ABSENCES. SIFT ROLE LINES. HANG THE OUTFIT ON THEM.

made marching girls with performer's hype and a fascination for uniform, a girl's protective militia to contain belonging longings, at least to flank the parade ground, its focal body ... till relinquishing stalls and gods she bags the wings and flies out of the board-game to risk unheard-of roles, unspoken acts, woken from trance

- Not me. I always identified with the prince - hacking through all those thorns, waking the princess...
- Me too! But I was getting out, not in - and I'm not sure I didn't leave her behind. In charge, of course.
- You didn't take her with you?
- Not then, not then. There were other things to get to. She had to catch up, the sleeper.

clueless, nightmare rider, rubbing fingermarks, footprints, bloodstains, smoothing out pinprick, sheets swears sacking, magnet of small change, kiddies crowsfeet, interest piling up columns, web of nervous threadworms along head-lines hot-lines clothes-lines place-lines -long long lines of silences

- Silence for The Marching Girls! This weeks focus is - da-dum - minorities!
- Genres within genres rise.

FILL IN A SILENCE ON THE BOTTOM LINE

The Marching Girls are pulling on their boots: they button their jackets, trickle out to the football paddock

- You really are in the middle of things up here. Don't you get paranoid about being overlooked?
- No more so than lower down.
- High living takes a literal interpretation. In default of the other kind.
- You mean a lack of bodily comfort might have compensations? A bit lofty aren't you?
- You need a Dickinson basket on a rope to let down with notes and cookies...
- Uh uh. Offerings only please. If they're acceptable the guest can come up too.
- But not via your new electrified haircut, Rapunzel ... is it shockproof?
- Well it only seems to shock at street-level. The atmosphere's more rarified up here. - The ivory tower at last
- More like Babel really ... the conversations between balconies are a hoot.

Not, maybe, high class but definitely not unearthly. Picture my next- floor neighbour speeding her overnighter off, then switching up to a tete-a-tete assessment hot off the .... well, what's a good bonk between storeys after all.

- Mixing the 'byes and 'lo's ...

The Marching Girls are recalcitrant; they mooch, they mutter, they huffle among each other, some stare others out

- And once I caught the world news live.
- Live?
- I'd come back from Club Mad and was talking to my garden -
- Does it talk back?
- Oh, sweet nothings and somethings ... perspectives on manic depressive minders and lesbian schiz... It doesn't go much on extremities - living and dying and how much should you pay for a Jasmine Oakley original, that sort of thing. Pot plants only accommodate you so far ... anyway, there I was out on the balcony pottering with the drinks and greetings and I happened to look up. Now usually there's a couple of floors lit up and these little figures going like this... and like this...

TRACE BETWEEN THE DOTS TO MAKE CONNECTIONS

sweeping between columns, lugging rubbish bags into lifts
jerking up louvres slamming down seats pinching nostrils over

fruit season splashes and dead stinks floating through the chemical squirts... wringing out cheesecloth sponging snail-trails over shiny tiles clattering buckets - buckets! old aluminium clunkers from years back in the milking shed but this liquid's cloudy, a thin undrinkable ward-milk smell oozes corridors stretching to deserts in a deserted dream set down where hallways open a forum on to the landing ... jabbing a grey spaghetti mophead into the corner leaving a damp glistening track, an arrowhead sign of the bucket carrier, the water-drawer, who changes rods in cultures, poles in centuries but not jobs, hands of the water-drawer spilling a bright moon-scalp stream

THIS FIGURE CLAIMED THE OLDEST CASTE EMBODIES SOME DISAGREEMENT ON ITS GENDER. STATE YOUR CHOICE. GIVE REASONS.

to step back for a change of tool
- and like this...
- Did you ever use one of those things?
- Yep. Awkward on the corners, tough on the ovaries and hell on the shins when you trip over the cord.

The Marching Girls watch one of their number stretch and split varying expressions

flick the flex swing from the hip so wrists don't jar and whine rise stalled handle the abdomen heave swivel and graunch off a sticky crab skid slide into a heavy-headed drone so no black rubbery scrapes on the lino don't crash the wall or scrabble the skirting-boards or judder and tip sideways and wrench the plug so the flex flops skitters a thin black coil a wizened umbilical cord so a body thrust steers brushes to the edges of swing doors to a landing drop where echoes float up the stairwells - voices, clanks, lift-hums

- It reminds me of one of those fourteenth century illustrations of Mount Purgatory. What sin were you expiating? Apart of course from being female.
- Probably poverty. Along with the rest of the crew... unless naivity's a sin?
- My theology doesn't stretch that far but these days I'd say yes.
- Mmm... I remember this one baleful night... we had a new young cleaner start, very shy, she was saving to go home and bring her child back - it cost as much to the islands then as to Europe - well, the supervisor was showing her how to handle the polisher and a bit snarky with it, you know, undercurrent stuff, and she switched the machine on before Renata got hold of it properly and - whoosh! Off

it went along the corridor, took off like a thing possessed, heading for the end room like a drunken homing pigeon...

HOW MANY VOICES MAKE A GLEE? IF THREE, SUGGEST ACCOMPANIMENT.

-... so the supervisor bangs off the wall switch and nothing happens - or rather, it keeps on happening - the machine goes zigzagging through the desks, barging into files and bins, knocking out cabinets - what a kerfuffle. So everyone stands there stupefied for a bit, then the supervisor grabs the plug to pull it out and gets blown back off her feet and someone goes haring down and everyone yells to leave it alone...
- Ha - Crazed Polisher Runs Amok. Sweeps Office Block Contents Into The Street, Documents Lost...
- Nearly. So somebody else pokes the plug with a broom and gets shocked and eventually somebody else goes for the mains and an electrician and we sit there in the dark for a while. Then some reporter gets in on the act ...
- Handlers Grip Goes Haywire. Covey of Night Cleaners Reel
- Not at all. More like: Supervisor Teresa Orr, 37, married with two children, expresses regret; she has "no idea how it happened" - but suspects
- Instant retribution?
- Subversion, more likely.
- Culture Shock?
- Cleaner Suilofa Ahai, married with five children says: "I couldn't beleive my eyes"; Renata Desu, 19, one child, described the incident as "frightening, the machine made its own life"; Katrina Dearsley, 30, solo mum, said it was hilarious, "like something out of a science fiction movie"; Edna Brown, 58, widow, said: "You won't get me on the back of one of those things again, next time it might take me"; Derek Buck, 23, part-time student, said "it could have been an overload of static electricity"; Dana Tamaera, 40, six children, said it was the funniest thing she'd seen: "Some cleaning maniac let loose" she told the reporter who wrote the story which a sub-editor cut to three sentences, Derek's theory, and a notification to the Department of Science Friction and Industrial Unrest. We laughed ourselves silly for weeks.

STUDY THE PICTURE. SPOT THE MISSING PERSONS. COLOUR BY NUMBER, STATUS, AND DISTRIBUTION.

The Marching Girls regroup and drill, two whisper back in the changing rooms, their uniforms are new with shiny buttons

- Well the issues are there. Sort of.
- And the characters aren't bad for a latish soap.
- Which one's the dyke?

- No, not the one in the jumpsuit, not the one who plays her, that one there.
- She's lovely.
- The busdriver's all right too.
- We're allowed to be human these days.
- Is human allowed to be woman?
- It's an up-to-date occupation. If somewhat restricted in its routes.
- No high rises from low places too suddenly.
- They might have chosen symbolically ... a plumber?
- ... a mechanic...
- ...a pychie nurse ...
- ... anthropologist, more like ...
- ... the inventor, the inventor ...
- But would they March?
- Not, perhaps, with the Girls.

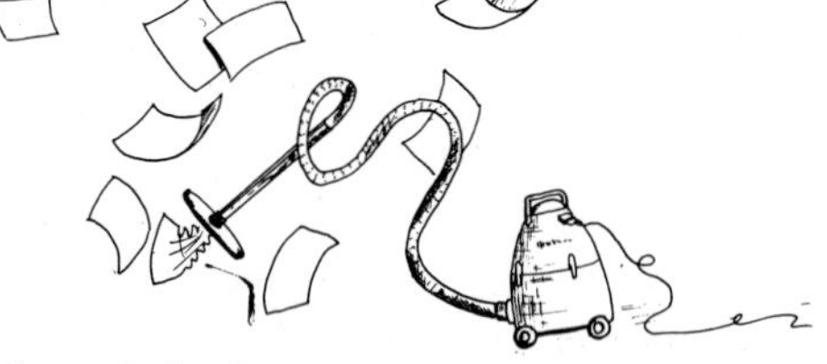

The Marching Girls relax, mock suitors, laugh in by-ways the misses pick, fade out into cleaning fluid ad

- Look, I was telling you about my world news night. Now we've got the cleaning done.
- Was the Life/Accident sign revolving round and round like that out the window then?
- What? Oh yes, a bit of contributory ambience you might say... well, this particular night, instead of just a couple of floors the whole building's lit up like a Christmas tree, and instead of little figures drudging up and down there's all these white shirt-sleeved bods hustling round and bending over ovens and darting from room to room going... and rushing up to each other with handfuls of papers going - Look!
-...?
- Something going on here I decided. So I turned the sound box on...

here, here take it this hot potato the night cleaners are under seige pause at alert mops at ease skirt paper carriers slip round scrum-backs a chorus let loose with props while lead roles take up the act

DEFINE SUSPECT CURRENCY, PRECARIOUS SECURITIES.

- the market crash!
- and the long drop set off here.
- A sickening stream, I'd say, having watched the play. Quite ... piquant, really. You've just seen x amount of dollars disappear...
- and your own lifestyle temporarily intact...
- Beware reverberations. Like an earthquake - the jolts go on for months, and the damages.

- And those with most reserves pick up most quickly. It hasn't disturbed the pyramid overmuch. No sad stories of the deaths of kings.

PINPOINT THE KINGPIN. HIS CLUE IS THE LARGEST CELL.

a huge lit disc, a hot-air balloon hangs globe-bellied, grinning in, its lineaments a face ... reception's not too good, interference jitters the lines, the director - or is it God? with Santa Claus beam and insistent beckoning forefinger fades to a staring Oscar eye pouches and confoundings, funny number beans sprout tumbling red and blackening out his mouthpiece

The Marching Girls sort factions and alliances; some hold to Colonel Bogey, some urge a pop-rock beat... military two-step, jazzercise? for fun? or to compete?

Where's the flanker call the retrievers whose is the sideways move? face, a featureless puffball, skews... too many darts fired in jerked out stabbed in a different place or the same revolving hole, no longer a static solid it's a wheel about to turn and hands grab out to catch it wrench back cruisers rearrange losers, but it's only a bit of cardboard after all... it drops quickens spins, it's spinning into a Catherine wheel

WHEN THE STOCKWHEEL HITS ROCK BOTTOM WHO DOES IT HURT?

- Add another few dollars on butcher's tags in the suburbs ... and bread goes up and jobs go down
- When the corporates tighten their belts and workers fall out the bottom
- Isn't the motto women and children first?

a Marching Girl argues hotly with her husband. She says: I'm the union rep, they picked me, I've got to go. He says: And who looks after the kids?

DESCRIBE THE HIERARCHY IN a) YOUR FIRST JOB b) YOUR LAST JOB c) YOUR PRESENT

a night cleaner waxing a counter works out food left after the bills, a night cleaner behind her mutters, low-toned, looking ahead: Think of the millions we've saved with no investments

- That's her doing a cartwheel in the background.
- Pretty fit.

- They said she didn't look butch enough for the part. And her hair's too long and anyway, they wanted someone dark.
- You mean at my age I've got to dye to fit the stereotype?
- The consumer image isn't exactly - authentic.
- She's courting in a properly retiring way.
- you mean she's made from projection not conviction.
- It's only the entree yet. Main course coming up - with any luck.

The Marching Girls swing into squadaerobics to the beat of Iron Lung

PLOT A PAPERCHASE IN YOUR LANDSCAPE. ON ONE SIDE CHART ITS DICHOTOMIES. ON THE OTHER ITS DISARRAY.

goods perch on a futurity branch roost with the courses O God O Lotto sparks tumble down down through twentyeight floors to hit verandah outcrops rattle stones scoria scorched models charred toys mansions with melted windows superstructure hung off iron piping, scaffolding exposed

a Marching Girl gone, unsanctioned, to a rock gig must now, to get home, choose between her boyfriend and her dad.

- Incest-survivors all. More wine?
- Mmm... most don't know.
- And those who do tucked into pockets of resistance.
- The queue for shock treatment is all female.
- Or brown.
- So's the informed - the sentient resistance.
- So do you break the cage or opt for a better zoo?

Dad's discovered a puncture; he and boyfriend get together over the jack and blocks.

COUNT YOUR STOCK ON THE REVOLVING WHEEL. WHOSE INTEREST? WHICH COLLECTORS?

stock in the basement with a banned label on the door, stock in the Square and the populace spitting fire, stock in a ward with electric shocks to short-circuit the connections, stock in the cell

START AT THE ENTRANCE TO THE MAZE AND TRACK THE TREASURE

- Untouchable to director in one generation? It's possible.
- With undistracted attention.
- You mean no kids.

- Oh, you can swing them too. Nannies, house-husbands, a godfather or two...
- Oh, there's precedent. No inevitability, precious little security and maybe an identity or two to juggle judiciously on the way...
- Depends what station you start from.
- Whose train you're pressed into...

cleaners bundle cast-offs for the shredder left-behind basins gleam malevolent show-host teeth paper cups with fold-in grins a death mask line to the backyard bay and lights dip, blink, to moth-startles, going out ... is it a dancer in the centre? with spiky hair streaming Saturn rings and snaky fire down long brown arms tossing fireballs and sizzling spheres - green blue violet purple red her coloured skirt melts the faster she spins

Daughter sits pretty in a great reconciliation; the busdriver's choice, met by nightclub, prefers men

- Well, our stocks may be low and our shares minimal but you can't say we're in danger of over-inflation.
- Not in the Marching Girls. Try a harder game - baseball?
- But not business.
- It isn't bankruptcy. Quite.
- Just keep thinking futurities, not commodities.
- I know which I'd rather have.
- Oh I'd plump for some nice gilt-edged securities myself. My own position tending to the skeletal. I mean commodities, not body-size.
- Anonyms don't appeal.
- Nor anorexia. If I couldn't be the little woman, I wasn't going to be the invisible dyke.
- A stake-out, not a burnt stake.
- Right. At least I meet the odd queer image - even if it's my own.
- Nice to have company though. On screen or off.
- Lots! Living happily - dare I say richly - ever after.
- I'd just fancy a bit more visible flesh. And much less blood.
- So... shall we go to the club?

behind a pipe band, clowns and sponsor's float, The Marching Girls lead Santa in the Christmas street parade

a flutter of fluorescent wing-flaps, floor by floor the stage goes dark the night cleaners head into streetlight pools a theatre of little stage-sets where wigged and hairless mannequins stuck in unnatural poses gaze into transcendental futures for displaced souls ... "bye... night...see ya...in the soup" the night cleaners spread to taxi stands and fifteen-hand battered cars, past malls and side street mazes to the highway to a key in the front-door porch and hallways with dark stuffy smells and sleepers grunts floating out half-open doors

NOMINATE YOUR FAVOURITE SOAP. SQUARE GLAMOUR TO THE POWER OF IMPOSITION.

downstairs Mariana's a rock-beat blast a slithery glitzy floor strobe-lit and extravagant, dancing women and mirror-backed bays, streaky faces luminous arms... tunic buttons, three big cops with lifted noses block the stairway

- ......!
- ...?
- I like..
- Shout!
- ...the reflective floor!

PAN OUT FROM THE CITY.

TAKE IN HARBOUR.

COASTLINE.

EXTEND TO SEA.

EXTEND INDEFINITELY.

cross-worlds dancers move in out gleams flax-skin eely blouse breasts jeans the music stops the dj's voice in a hollow aura warns: Remember... her caution floats, unsaid, the women's voices buzz lift

- I see the force still let us know that they're in charge.
- Visibility - on its own - being no protection. I see we lack some natural ease towards intrusion.
- Something to do with size?
- Or habits of independence.

- Or resources in high places. I mean their lack.
- Well God's self-made. He knows the self-made woman won't stop here. And others hear.
- He's only terrified of his origins being sprung. Having usurped his mother's attributes and power he's got to stamp out heresy. It's not just rules being flouted, it's the game.
- And this is the front-line here? Well, blow me dancing days...
- Not the dancing, dear, the partners.
- You know what they do with clubs.
- I'd rather not...
- This is a glimpse of your futurities. Only with spokeswomen ...
- ... for the spokes?
- ... instead of brokers, I was going to say ...
- ... for the possibilities!
- Why not the hub?

INVENT A BOARDGAME THAT THROWS OUT THE BACON AND OPTS FOR INDIGO. MIX PIE SLICE, KAI MOANA, RICE. SAFEGUARD FROM MARAUDERS, FALLOUT, BACKLASH.

a glittering bird-woman flies off, Mariana's spins a whirlpool, an underground well, dancers become wordsmiths horsewomen chanters, transform, the coloured spots among white shirt brokers beetling into high-rise combs

COMPARE YOUR BOTTOM LINE WITH YOUR FRIENDS. THE NEIGHBOURS. THE CLEANING LADIES. CALCULATE COSTS.

in view of cells that issue identities, securities, time-payment, stocks and power and inaccessible shares...

- ...?
- I'm remembering my displaced youth. Shall we dance?

Lesbian Videos - Seen Any Lately?

Sally Smith

How choosey are you? I went looking for lesbian films, and was actually surprised at the number I found. What did not surprise me was the number I didn't want to see. I put all the films into various categories:-
1 Enjoyable

Films with mainly lesbian content, showing positive images of lesbians, which are currently available. If you haven't seen *Desert Hearts* and *Personal Best*, you've only just come out, or you are living in the country. In either case, I advise you to take a trip to the city and see these films.

2 Frustrating

Generally available films with one or more brief appearances by lesbians, in a positive, or relatively neutral way. Some of these may be a surprise to you - keep that finger ready on the rewind button. *Manhatten* - Woody Allen loses Meryl Streep to another woman, *The Group* - Lakey returns from Europe, *Once Is Not Enough* - Jacqueline Susann's novel is adapted to film and shows a warm lesbian relationship, *A Perfect Couple* - Robert Altman's film with an unobtrusively integrated happy lesbian couple, *Five Easy Pieces* - with Jack Nicholson and Karen Black as the straight couple who pick up a couple of hitchhiking funny lesbian ecology enthusiasts, *A Wedding* - another Robert Altman movie where the wedding caterer kisses the bride, (don't blink or you'll miss it), *X, Y, and Zee* - where Elizabeth Taylor and Susannah York make love, *California Split* - with a lesbian waitress, *Sammie and Rosie Get Laid* - several minor characters, (not particularly likeable characters, but refreshingly real), *Lenny* - a woman with lesbian tendencies.

3. Rather Confusing

Generally available films with strong positive images of women in which the lesbianism has been deleted. You probably know about *The Colour Purple* where a major relationship, and integral part of the story is reduced to a single kiss, but did you know about *My Brilliant Career*? This too was a lesbian story in the book, but got completely deleted when it made it to the big screen. *Nine to Five* the women could/should have been lesbians, and in *Celine et Julie vont en Bateau (Celine and Julie Go By Boat)* we see two women identified characters, but without any overt sexuality. In another French film *Diaboliques* - a very good (if old, made in 1955) horror suspense film, the screenplay was originally written with lesbian characters, which were deleted. Then of course, there's the old stars of Hollywood, with films like *Morocco* - with Marlene Deitrich, and *Queen Christina* - with Greta Garbo, you might get to see in a film festival.

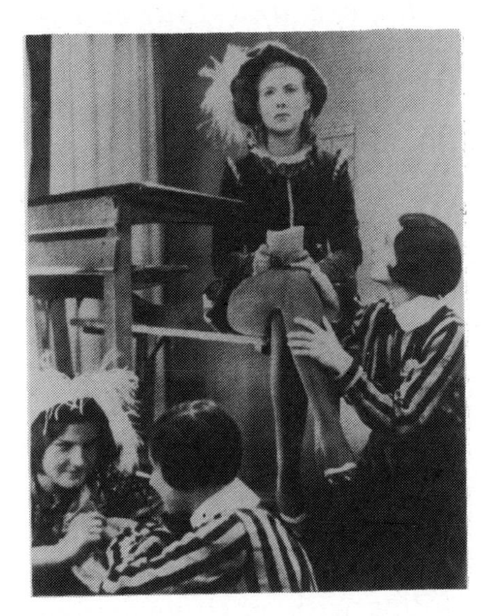

4 The Truly Terrible

And they really are, and they are not even any good for a laugh. What's worse there are so many of them. If you are really desperate to see a lesbian on video, watch *Desert Hearts* again (okay, I know it's the fifteenth time) but don't watch this trash. The only interesting thing about these films is that it shows what a taboo subject lesbianism is, since it can only be shown, after it has been established how awful the character really is. This is done in the widest possible variety of ways. *From Russia with Love* - the evil killer dyke, *Walk On The Wild Side* - lesbian pimp, *Lilith* - mental patient, *The Fox* - where one lesbian is murdered and one becomes heterosexual, *The Silence*- incestuous sisters, - *Scrubbers* - lesbians in jail, *Cleopatra Jones* - dope pushers and gang leaders, *The Children's Hour* - lesbian suicide, *Olivia* - brave teacher represses her unhealthy desire for one of her pupils, *Twice a Woman* lesbianism induces panic, *Emmanuelle* - soft porn, *Flesh* - Andy Warhol puts lesbians in as part of a freak show, and *Blood and Roses* - lesbian vampire.

5. Only Just Bearable

Films which show lesbians in fairly negative ways, but which may be worth seeing for other reasons, if you can stand it. *The Hunger* is a

lesbian vampire movie, of excellent quality, with powerful major lesbian characters. *The Killing of Sister George* - actually an interesting study of rather odd personalities, its just a shame that the oddness is explained by the lesbianism.
Therese and Isabelle - an equal, loving and sexual relationship between two young women. It's a pity it's told in flashback as one of them gets married.
Girlfriends is a mediocre film generally, and lesbianism is mentioned deliberately in order to deride it. At least it's mainly about a woman.
*The Children's Hour*is quite an oldie now, and shows a woman killing herself rather than be a lesbian. It's interesting in the light that Lillian Hellman wrote the screenplay, and it's real theme is the power of a lie to destroy lives, based on her experiences in the McCarthy era in the USA. (What about the power of a lying film to ...?)
Finally there's *The Rose* and *Julia* both of which contain pretty direct anti-lesbian messages, but which I know many people enjoyed despite this.

6. What A Tease

Films with positive images of lesbians as major characters which aren't available yet. Yes, they do exist, so keep your eyes open. *The War Widow* - lesbian as a survivor who then moves to the big city, and *A Question of Love* - a happy lesbian couple (both these movies were made for TV in the USA).
Comedy in 6 Unnatural Acts and *Home Movie* - Jan Oxenberg movies from the USA, *She Must Be Seeing Things* - English, recently made and explores a lesbian relationship, *Erika's Passions* - about lesbian lovers and *Rubyfruit Jungle* - which is in production. (True!)

Happy Hunting.

EUGENIA

The story of a woman who cross-dressed for most of her life has just been published. The book makes fascinating reading as it is one of the few accounts of a working class woman's survival by cross-dressing, and her relationships with women.
In 1920 a 45-year-old Italian woman, Eugenia Falleni was arrested for the murder of a woman three years earlier. The investigation led to the revelation of a woman who had lived for at least 20 years as a man.

Eugenia was born in Livorna, Italy, in 1875 and two years later her family immigrated to New Zealand. The Fellinis settled in Wellington and produced a large family, 22 children with 17 surviving. Eugenia was the eldest and grew up as a restless and undisciplined child. She was dark and strong and unwilling to learn to read and write. She was considered 'simple' and her tomboyishness was considered harmless. From an early age she was given to dressing in boys' clothes and running away from home. Sometimes she took jobs as a boy such as in the brick yards and in a laundry.

In her teens she ran away to sea as a boy. Her family did not hear from her for some years until at 23 years old she gave birth to a baby girl, Josephine Fellini. It was noted in later records that Eugenia had been 'violently used' by the captain of a ship she was working on and came ashore to Sydney to give birth. She gave her baby to an Italian woman Mrs De Anglais of Double Bay.

Soon after this, dressed in men's clothes and under the name Harry Crawford, Eugenia took a series of unskilled jobs as factory hand and hotel 'useful'. In 1913 she married Annie Birkett who had set up a little confectionery shop. The relationship was fractious with 'Harry' drinking and being abusive. The shop failed and they were apart for some time but 'Harry' was still a frequent visitor. By 1916 they were living together again and 'Harry's' daughter Josephine came to live with them, with Annie accepting that 'Harry' was Josephine's father.
Unfortunately for Annie, Josephine was pestered by the neighbours as to the whereabouts of her mother. Josephine, in a fit of exasperation blurted out,

"There's my mother over there, dressed up as a man." The neighbours couldn't resist telling Annie, who discussed it with her sister. She talked about having her marriage annulled but on September 1917 she set off with 'Harry' for a picnic and was never seen alive again. It was three years before Eugenia was arrested and charged with the murder of Annie Birkett and even at the trial, at least one woman lover could not believe that she was other than a man. Eugenia was convicted and sentenced to Long Bay prison from where she was released in 1929.
Eugenia: A Man by Suzanne Falkiner
Pan Books, Sydney & London 1988
ISBN 0-330-27112-1

DANCING WITH STRINGS

A New Zealand Press has finally taken the risk and published a lesbian novel. While the lesbian community may not think it *is* a risk we have to remember that New Zealand's three million people, inspite of buying more books per head of population than most other nations, does not provide a large lesbian market. The first lesbian novel, *The Godmothers* by Sandi Hall, was published by the British Women's Press. Papers Inc. the small lesbian publishing group, can only keep producing lesbian books by maintaining a sexual abuse catalogue which is how it keeps its head above water. While Papers Inc. pays contributors and artists it does not pay for the day-to-day distribution, planning, word processing, proof reading, and marketing which is carried out by volunteers.
So we take our hat off to New Women's Press for publishing *Dancing With Strings* and hope that with its success we will see more.

Miriam Saphira, who wrote the first non-fiction lesbian book *Amazon Mothers*,to be published in New Zealand talked to Frances Cherry about *Dancing With Strings*.

"I didn't think about it being a lesbian novel. I just wrote where I was at. I didn't consciously think about an audience. I got carried away with something that was real for me.
"There have been plenty of people who could have written a New Zealand lesbian novel. I just think its the fear. Women are frightened of exposing themselves. As a writer you have to write about what you know, and be prepared to expose yourself. It's no good disguising it. I mean, in the book of short stories, *The Daughter-in-law and other stories*, I made a lesbian story into a heterosexual one. Mary Paul came to me and said it was a pity that I didn't have a lesbian story in the collection. When I said that one of the stories had been a lesbian story originally she suggested that I change it. I was worried that people would get the wrong impression. I did not want them to

think badly about lesbian relationships. I didn't want them to get the wrong idea. Now I think you can't try and make things sound good if it aren't. It's got to be real. If you contrive a situation people don't like it. Everybody knows relationships are not always easy and when you write realistically people accept it well. If you write about problems, good or bad, people see that in a lot of ways they are similar to what they have experienced.

"I write for myself. I'm not going to try and please any particular audience. I don't even have a particular market in mind. When its published I hope <u>everyone</u> will read it.

"I start writing and it just flows. I don't think to myself I'd better not put this in because this sort of person will read it, or that sort of person will read it, or I want that sort of person to think this. For all I knew lesbians might have been upset by the book but it hasn't turned out that way. Everybody, all sorts of people, lesbians included, have really enjoyed it. Most people have said that they couldn't put it down. The amazing thing is the different types of people (even a few men) have liked the book. A gay friend in Sydney- his mother had sent him a copy- rang to say he had thought it was wonderful and just had to ring to tell me.

"I think having parents who were different made me stronger. My parents were communists so Katherine's childhood is fairly autobiographical. (*Dancing With Strings* begins by describing Katherine's childhood as the daughter of two politically active communists in New Zealand).

"I was so used to being different it wasn't so difficult for me to accept my lesbianism. Then again I haven't always felt I was a lesbian. I felt confident, I had a sense of self worth. If you don't have that it's much more difficult.

"I loved giving my husband's Rotary friends a shock by telkling them my parents were communists.So I don't mind my book being acclaimed a lesbian novel. I want people to <u>think</u>. I wouldn't have written it if it wasn't to do with me. I <u>will</u> take a risk. I think that's what a writer has to do. I don't think you can be <u>careful</u>. It's scarey but you have to take that risk. I want to make people sit up and think about lots of things. I want to throw things at them, not be careful and tread around things, or pretend.

"It's funny but I've found people accept things quite well when you are straight forward. I thought some of the people in my class, especially some of the older ones would be shocked but weren't. One woman said her husband was buying it for her birthday, - I don't think he knows what sort of book it is though, she said. The book allows them to talk quite freely. If you don't say anything, they won't say anything because they don't want to upset you. People don't know how to broach the subject. If you talk openly they feel that they can, even if they say something a bit stupid. It gives you the opportunity to say, well, I don't think that's quite right. If it is mentioned naturally it allows for a free discussion. I have some people in classes who react a bit heavily. "I am a lesbian," and almost waiting for a reaction and it puts people on the defensive and ignores the rest of you.

"I think its important for people to know that lesbians are not always the stereotype, that they are just ordinary people who do ordinary things like they do. In a way that's why I still wear make up and want to wear makeup. It shows that all sorts of people can be lesbians. They don't have to wear big boots, grey clothes or conform to some kind of stereotype. Lesbians don't have to be frightening and heavy, they can/do look 'normal'.

In *Dancing With Strings* you don't know why the woman is on the beach. So the reader is trying to work out what is going on. There is a hint that something has happened to her. Parts are written in the second person to show the distance. Someone in a bad way is distanced from herself. You talk to yourself when you are needy....

"And running along with that is the past. But they are both going forward. They are both leading the reader on and the mystery is still not solved. You still don't know. When she starts to get better the 'you' turns to 'I'.

"I think that a first novel is always a bit autobiographical. You sort of take your life and then say what if... It's not the whole person. You take a small piece say sadness and accentuate it. You know what it is like to be miserable about something, so you put a character into a situation where they are miserable but you haven't put all the other things about you into it so it is not really you. I put this woman on the beach by herself. I haven't ever lived alone like that but I'd like to do it, see whether I could stay without a phone all by myself. I think it would be very interesting. That's the good thing about writing - you can create any life you want."

A Day In The Life Of

Mil Gibson.

Min's eyes opened to gold fingers of sun creeping round the edges of the bedroom blind.
How gold the sun really was in the early morning... Clearly golden... bright, light gold... warm, mellow gold...gold. The word lingered.
Funny about words - say one often enough in sequence and it lost all meaning, all sense; became merely a sound. Who first decided that the sound 'gold' should be a word, she wondered. She mentally rolled the word gold round in her mouth.
Even as she mused, the gold was waning to a paler yellow. And who, she wondered as she watched the fading colour had declared that yellow should be called yellow and gold called gold...
She moved her gaze to the ceiling. Such ponderings, she decided, could send her quietly mad. But then, what was 'mad'?
She was quite relieved when at last she felt Thyme stirring beside her in the bed.

"You know what ?" she said out loud, "I think those two cracks in the ceiling are opening up wider."
She knew Thyme was awake. The first thing Thyme ever did when she awoke was to rub her nose, and Thyme had just, quite vigorously, rubbed her nose. Min waited.
"Really? Interesting," Thyme mumbled, without much conviction, before turning to bury her face deeply in her pillow. "Shouldn't be surprised if we looked up one night and saw stars through those cracks," Min persisted, disregarding Thyme's apparent lack of interest, "and every time a car goes past half a ton of dust falls down. You are in danger, sleeping on your back with your mouth open. I think this house is slowly sliding down to the street. Maybe we should jack it up at the front and squeeze all the cracks back together again."
Thyme lifted her face from the pillow and glared up at the ceiling for a few seconds before turning to look at Min, who was still evaluating the potential fall-out from above.
"Jeez, you exaggerate," Thyme offered at last.
"You won't say that when you wake up one night with the ceiling in your mouth."
"Better than feet," Thyme muttered, and then, louder, "and I do not sleep with my mouth open!"
"Yes you do. You always have. I just haven't liked to mention it before. Anyway," Min suddenly sat up, taking most of the coverings with her, "it got your attention, didn't it..."
Thyme reached over, tugging what covers she could back around herself. "I can think of better ways of getting my attention first thing in the morning."
Min yawned, widely and noisily, before half turning to look down at Thyme.

"Cute!" she said. "I'll go and find someone with the necessary energy to give you the attention you require. Look, woman - look at these arms - ." She held her arms out above Thyme.
"Look! Visible evidence of what is happening to the rest of me! I'm like one of those left over party balloons, all wrinkly and loose - ."
"I kind of like loose women," Thyme interrupted.
"Let's face it, dear," Min went on, " the spring has long been sprung and the limber lumbered. Do you know I even pulled a muscle just turning down the covers last night. And when I move my joints sound like a collective celebration for November the fifth." She paused, letting her arms fall lifelessly down on to the bedcovers in front of her. "That ceiling has nothing on me."
Thyme laughed and pulled Min down to her. "You'll still do me," she said. "And even if your joints do sound like a bunch of fire crackers, its a sort of homely sound."
"Oh, your lovely turn of phrase," Min mumbled, as she nudged down warmly against Thyme's shoulder. How could the young woman inside this sere body fail to respond to such silver- tongued flattery."
"But you do talk too much - sometimes," Thyme murmured, her arms tightening around Min.
Min pressed her face gently against Thyme's clean-smelling curly grey hair. "And the sun is golden in the early morning," she said, softly.

"Let us go forth and permeate some excitement today."
They were sitting together outside on the plank seat Min had made the summer before, their backs resting against the house wall.
"Such as?" Thyme bit into a piece of toast and picked up her cup from the tray beside her feet.
"Blowing our pensions on something we don't need."
"Be nice, but it's not pension day until next week - or had you forgotten..." Thyme spoke thickly through toast crumbs and peanut butter.
"I had. Damn!" There was disappointment in Min's voice. She stared with mock forlorn at the narrow yellow leaves of the privet hedge beside them, then, brightening, and turning to Thyme, "I know - lets hijack a bus and take all those lonely looking over-burdened women we see dragging themselves around the supermarket out on a picnic."
"Too cold yet," Thyme said, "besides, Rosie's coming this afternoon."
"Oh. Well, let's take Rosie to the gardens and we'll hijack their shuttle bus. We can see the gardens, save your feet, and give Rosie the thrill, all at the same time."
Thyme placed her cup back down on the tray, brushed crumbs from her lap and stared in a good humouredly slightly bemused way at her partner.
"Mignonette Miranda, you do get some crazy ideas at times. Anyway, the shuttle service isn't running yet, and do you want this last piece of toast?" She held out the plate with the toast on it but Min shook her

head and wandered off around the corner of the house, followed in close file by Friendly and Dear One, their two marmalade cats.
Thyme inspected the toast, balanced the calorie intake against her own needs, then, breaking the toast into small pieces, she cast the bits over the ground. "Come, birds," she called, "break bread with us and I will have the wine."

There was one corner of their garden Min and Thyme favoured most. Under the large protective arms of an ageless gnarled apple tree, they had grown a peaceful resting space of soft feather-topped grasses, bordered by tiny, delicately rustling, bamboo and green ferns, and encircled by native toi toi and elegantly striped yellow and green flax. Within the privacy of their natural shelter they sat, with Thyme's grand-daughter, Rosie. A mild, late spring sun, cast a comfortable warmth over them as they spread around on a thick-piled old rug among the grasses, Thyme leaned her back against the old tree trunk, Rosie, her chubby legs curled beneath her, nestled in against her grandmother's lap, and Min, leaning back on one elbow, held Rosie's wide-eyed attention with a story.
"So, there were these two grandmothers," Min was saying, "who lived and loved for a thousand years - "
"Not me!" Thyme interrupted, firmly. "You know what you can do with your thousand years!"
"- who lived and loved for a thousand years," Min went on, ignoring Thyme's outburst. "And between them they had eighty-five children, two hundred and thirty grandchildren and four hundred and thirty-eight great grandchildren."
"Were some of the children called Rosie?" Rosie queried.
"And - would you believe - three hundred of them were named Rosie? Then there were one hundred named Thyme, fifty named Fern, forty named Mignonette, as well as twenty Verbena's, twenty Poppy's, twenty Lilliums and thirty Briars. Then, there were - let's see -" Min pretended to do a quick count on her fingers. "That's right. Then there were forty Daisys, ten Hollys, ten Daphnes, ten Celandines and eight Marigolds. There, what do you think about that?"
"I think you've missed out on about ninety-five," Thyme said drily.
Min pulled a face as she lay back to stare up at a clear blue patch of sky showing through the greening branches above. "Oh, yes - well they were all named Basil, " she allowed. "And were they all happy?" Rosie asked, not wanting to let go of the story.
"Oh yes. Mostly they were happy. Well, they had so much to do that they didn't have time to be unhappy. They had their animals to look after, because, of course, they had lots of animal friends - then there were the vegetables and fruit to grow because they had to eat, and, of course, they couldn't eat their animal friends -"
"Like Dear One and Friendly?"
"Like Dear One and Friendly, and the cows and goats they had for

milk, and the sheep for wool - And they wove and sewed and knitted and painted pictures and made music and told stories. And they built places to live in and danced and talked and sometimes they'd argue - just a little - about who had eaten the last of the plum jam and not washed the bowl -"
"And who was going to do the dishes?" from Rosie.
"Oh no, they never bothered wasting time arguing about silly things like that," said Min. "They had far more important things to do."
"Like shed roofs?" Thyme suggested, quietly.
Min gave an exaggerated sigh. "Now you've spoiled it all, and I was just getting to the really interesting part."
"Go on, go on, Min -" Rosie pleaded.
"Sorry, Rosie." Min slowly sat up, "but your grandmother's quite right. Shed roofs are important too. Especially one as noisy as ours. It makes great gusty, rusty, groaning noises every time the wind blows, and horrible wet flapping sounds when it rains." She eased herself up onto her feet, stretching stiffly, then held her hand down to Rosie. "Come on - I'll need your help to carry the ladder, then you can watch while I put the poor roof out of its pain."
"Nana -"
Thyme looked down into Rosie's violet eyes."
"Can I get up on the shed roof with Min?"
"No, Rosie, you might fall through."
"But Min isn't falling through. Can I though, please -"
"Rosie put one chubby hand on the ladder that was leaning against the ageing grey wood of the shed. "Please, Nana? I could hold the nails for Min."
"No, Rosie, not today." There was a gentle firmness in Thyme's voice. Your mum wasn't too happy last time when you went home with paint all over you, remember?"
The child pouted slightly. "But that was 'n accident because I tripped over when Min was painting the fence."
Min's round tanned face suddenly appeared over the edge of the roof. "Don't nag, Rosie. It makes your grandmother's feet ache when you nag."
Rosie looked with instant curiosity, down at Thyme's feet then up into her face. "Does it, Nana? Does it make the ritis worse in your feet?"
"Of course it does," Min said. "Everyone knows that nagging is bad for arthritis. Now you help your Nana to lift that long piece of wood up so that I can reach it -"
Together the child and the older woman balanced a long wide plank, lifting it in the air towards Min, Rosie giggling at Min's first abortive attempt to reach it.
"Now you can make a nice muddy hole to put our new shrub in, Rosie," Min called, the plank and herself safely settled on the roof.
Rosie peered up at Min, excitement edging her voice as she shouted, "Have you got it? Have you got my new tree? What's it called, Min?"

"Why Rosemary of course, what else?" Min called back.

"Now gently, gently -" Thyme bent down beside Rosie, taking the child's small muddy hands in hers and guiding them over the balled roots of a young plant. "These are the plant's tender little roots and we're going to gently pull them free so they can spread out and grow." The child's small fingers carefully followed the movements of the larger, more capable hands of her grandmother; timorous, tentative little proddings, slowly gaining in confidence as each root tendril was freed and spaced out around the damp soil.
"Now," Thyme slowly straightened, "we make sure that it's nice and even, then we'll cover the wee roots with this warm crumbly earth. Here -"she held back the springy dark greenery with one hand, "you help me now to cover it, like this," and with her free hand she deftly moved the soil in around the plant, and Rosie, squatting happily beside her, patted and smoothed, an intent serious look on her small child face.

From her vantage point, up on the shed roof, Min looked down and across the section to where Rosie and Thyme were admiring their handiwork. The small figure, dressed in fawn bib overalls, muddy little hands at her sides, leaned against that of the older woman. Thyme was talking quietly, explaining to Rosie how the leaves did the breathing for the plant, how nature knew it's own way. "Of course, they don't really need us," Thyme was saying, "but we need them, and when we take a little plant like this into our garden, then we should always take care to look after it properly."
Rosie studied the shrub for a short space, then looked up at Thyme. "But Nana, if they don't really need us, why do we have to look after them?"
"Because we choose to have them, they don't choose to have us, so we should take care of them, and when we plant them in our gardens in the city there are all sorts of things in the air that plants don't like."
"Like flies?" Rosie questioned, her face turned seriously up to Thyme.
Thyme laughed. "No, flies don't really bother them, but there's grimy dust and petrol fumes, and sometimes thoughtless people use nasty sprays and all these things settle on the plants' leaves and they can't breathe properly. Just like when you have a cold and your nose gets all stuffy, you know? So we can wash the plant's leaves with the hose and give it a cool drink of water when its thirsty - and we can love it. That's most important. They please us because we like to look at them and touch them and smell them - "
"Will it grow as big as me?"
"Just as big and probably just as fast." Thyme placed a comfortable hand on Rosie's shoulders. "And remember, you can come and tell it how much you love it whenever you feel like it, and later, when its a

bit bigger, it will bloom all over with pretty blue flowers and then the bees will come to it to do their gathering."

A time for all things and each to its own time, Min mused, as she turned from watching, a smile on her lips. Her back ached and her legs felt wobbly from too long kneeling on the roughly uneven roof, but there, she'd done her best and at least, for a while, the shed would be rain-proof. All she had to do now was to get back down again without Thyme seeing how stiffly she was moving. She eased her body over to the edge of the shed, dropped the hammer to the ground and began slowly and carefully to descend the ladder.

Min lifted the lid from the large pot of vegetable stew simmering on the stove and scooped out a wide spoonful, blowing on it until it cooled enough to taste. "Mmm - ". She exaggerated a display of tasting. "Think it might need a touch more of something."
"Something what?" Thyme came up behind her and reaching over, took the spoon from Min and tasted what was left on it.
"Tastes fine to me."
"Still needs something, " Min insisted.
"Well you find your something and put it in - as long as it isn't more garlic," Thyme added.
"Okay." Min moved over to their shelf of herbs, running her finger along the edge until she came to what she wanted. "Can I taste?" Rosie, standing between them, waited expectantly.
"Oh, sorry love. Here - ," Min scooped out another spoonful and handed it to Rosie. "But wait until it's cool or it will burn your sweet lips and make them look like old tarpaper."
"What's old tarpaper?"
"The stuff I was putting on the shed roof, and we wouldn't want your wee mouth to look like the old shed roof now, would we?"

Rosie tentatively touched the tip of her tongue to the spoon, then opened her mouth and let the food slide in. "Mmm - " she wiped the back of her hand across her mouth and held the spoon up for more. "Can I stay for tea?"

"Not today, Rosie," Min said, handing her another spoonful.
"Your mum's coming at four."
"She could stay too."

"No," Thyme was bent over a bowl, washing kumara, "she's going to a meeting tonight so she wants you home early."
"Mum's always going to meetings." There was a sulk in Rosie's voice.
"Yes, of course she is," Min chided lightly, " because your mum's a people and its good for people to be interested in all sorts of things. You wouldn't want your mum to stay around the house all the time and grow lumpy and mouldy would you?"
Rosie gave a quick gurgle of laughter. "Lumpy and mouldy," she shouted "just like bread pud!"
"Why lumpy and mouldy?" Thyme asked in an aside to Min.

"Oh, I don't know, it seemed as good as anything else." As she spoke there was a light tapping on the outer door followed by Fern calling hallo. Rosie raced from the kitchen to greet her mother, tugging at her hand as they crowded back through the doorway.
"Min said you could grow lumpy and mouldy and we planted a tree for me and Friendly and Dear One scratched up all nana's seeds-"
Fern hugged Rosie to her, quietening her and smiling down at her face. "I may grow lumpy, little toot, but never mouldy. Not with you around, anyway."
"Not while we're around, either," Min said. First sign of mould and we'll have you stripped down faster than you can say paint stripper."
Fern laughed and moved over to look into the pot of stew. She drew in a deep breath of appreciation and Min handed her the spoon they had all been using. They watched, waiting, as Fern in her turn tasted.
"Delicious," she declared at last. "How do you two manage it? Every one a winner."
Min and Thyme laughed. "We don't know," Min confessed. "It just works out that way."
"We never really know what it's going to be like," Thyme added.
"We put in whatever we have to hand and hope."
"Nana and me planted my tree," Rosie piped, in an effort to regain her mother's attention.
"Oh?" Fern placed the spoon in the sink and turned back to her daughter. "What kind of tree?"
"A Rosemary, of course, what else?"

Together Min and Thyme gathered the used dishes from the table and carried them out to the kitchen.
The last rays of the early evening setting sun filtered through the louvres above the sink bench, painting long narrow lengths of pale yellow light across the kitchen wall. Min filled a wash bowl with hot soapy water and Thyme dropped the dishes into it. They worked in amicable silence through the chore of washing and drying until Min, as she was wiping down the bench, asked Thyme "How are your feet?"
"They're fine," she said, her back to Min.
"Liar!" Min accused.

"Why?" asked Thyme.
"Why a liar, or why about your feet?"
"Both."
Well, for one, your feet could drop off and you'd push them away out of sight rather than let me know and, two, I thought that if they weren't too painful we could go for a short stroll through evening suburbia."
"Of course."
"Of course, what?"
"We can go for a walk."
"You sure?"
"Sure I'm sure."
"Right, then let's go."

They were walking down the darkening narrow street on the last block back to their house. Two middle-aged women, hands casually linked, their steps slowing as they neared their corner. Suddenly Min stopped, pulling Thyme, to a halt beside her. "Look!" She put an arm around Thyme , pulling her close and directing her attention to a mass of pure white blossom crowded into a small space between other dusking shrubs.
"Oh, Thyme, isn't it beautiful - Hold on, I'll see if I can reach a piece. After all - " she stretched out across the paling fence, "I'm sure such beauty is meant to be shared, and a little bit of pruning never does any harm - "
Thyme held Min steady as she strained to break a small trembling bloom from it's springy branch.
"There!" Min regained her balance and held the fragrant white flowerlet out to Thyme, and Thyme, taking it from Min's hand, impulsively leaned over and kissed Min on the mouth. As they kissed, their bodies held apart, protecting the blossom Thyme held between them, a car hurtled by and through the open car windows shouts came at them, "Old dykes... screwing old lezzies -" The obscenities spewed out as, with a scream of tyres, the car circled around on the roadway, roaring up close to where they stood on the footpath. A bottle was thrown from the car and crashed, shattering glass around their feet, before the car zoomed off up the street.

"Puking little peckers!" Min raged, seeing the angry shock on Thyme's face. "Sometimes - just sometimes, I could - "
"Could what?" Thyme asked.
Min looked down at the broken glass around their feet.
"I don't know," she said despairingly. "I don't know. Just try to go on living I suppose."
Among the sharp cuts of glass, where it had fallen, lay the blossom.

Min stooped and gently picked it up. Cupped in her hand it seemed to have lost the white purity that it had held before. Somehow, it now looked almost ... dirtied.

Yellow from the outside overhead street light seeped round the edges of the bedroom blind.
Min lay on her back in the dark, staring up at the cracks winding their black trails across the ceiling.
The night was as still as a silent pool across which rippled the distant sounds of late moving traffic.
Another day marked off the calendar of all the days that had been.
How many days in sixty-two years? It was of no matter. One day at a time was all they had. One hour, one minute, this one instant of breathing time .
Thyme lay sleeping quietly beside her. Thyme of the clean- smelling curly grey hair, and eyes that changed colour with the changing light; one light moment deepening brown, one changing light moment dark hazel.
Min slid one hand down between them, and Thyme, sensing rather than being consciously aware of the movement, reached over and curled her fingers around Min's.
They lay together, wrapped around by their warm cloak of caring, of understanding, of loving, and of - just knowing.

Mil Gibson.

BREAKFAST IN BED
I'm going to give you breakfast in bed this morning my love
ahhh - how lovely
snuggle
HEY! where's the coffee?
Its on the stove!
oh! The bloody grill won't work!!
Try turning it on at the wall!
eh?
TRY TURNING IT ON AT THE WALL!
cont...

9
Oh, I can't find the butter anywhere!
10
Never mind!
I'll get my bloody breakfast myself!
11

RITUALS

It was a dark and stormy night. The wind blew through the carrot patch, rippling round the beetroot, and blowing against the bean brakes. Marva crouched near the pumpkins watching Willa crawling on hands and knees into the corn. Her backside gleamed snowy white in the moonlight. Marva admired the view.

Her knees ached. She shifted position. The sodden satin pillow stuck to her breasts as she shifted and peeled it away. The cool, moisture laden wind breathed across her nipples. She shivered as they hardened. Willa was almost out of sight, just flashes of silver flesh glimmering among the corn stalks.

"Okay, I'm ready." The husky whisper blew back to Marva, tattered and breathy. A dark cloud mass crawled over the moon. Marva dug nervously around the near row of carrots, pulling up several. She started to wipe them on the pillow, then remembered and rubbed the earth on her thigh instead.

"Come on, come on. " Willa's impatient voice floated over the corn rows. Marva couldn't see anything now, no moon, no flash of silver skin, no scary shadows. She clutched the satin pillow and crawled over the pumpkin vines. The corn stalks rustled crisply like new dollar bills, beckoning Marva on.

"Where are you? Willa, I can't see anything."

"I'll light the candles when you get here." Willa's whisper seemed to come from the left. Marva crawled into the corn. The earth crumbled damply under hands and feet.

"Where?" she called.

"Here ..." A dark form loomed.

Marva still couldn't tell exactly where Willa's voice was. She groped for the dark form and found a foot. She had grabbed an ankle before she realized that the foot was shod.

A bright light flashed, blinding her. She froze like any frightened rabbit.

"Good God!" exclaimed Farmer Jones patriarchally, bending over her scared moon face. "What's going on here?"

Marva stared up, trying to think of a reasonable explanation for two women crawling naked around a vegetable patch.

She clutched the sodden pillow to her and held up a shaking hand. "Have a carrot stick," she said.

Nancy Peterson

MAGIC MOMENTS, OR A TRUE RITUAL WOMAN

" Has everyone brought an instrument? Good. You're so inventive." Mindy smiles, bright eyed at the assembled women. "I'm going out of the room now. When you hear me playing a tune on my pipe I want you Jodie to turn off the light and then everyone make as much noise as you can with your instruments." Mindy disappears.
The women wait expectantly for the music. Nothing happens. They look at each other. Jodie begins to grin. Fay tries not to notice, to look serious.
"Maybe I should turn the light off anyway," says Jodie and the room is plunged into darkness. Fay feels Jodie's fingers brushing against her white robe. She feels incredibly spiritual. She's not sure if it's the folds of old cotton sheeting flowing over her naked body, or the energy moving from Jodie's fingers to her solstice gown.
I'll go and see what's happened." Margaret turns on the light and leaves the room. Fay can't understand why Margaret comes to this group. She's so cynical, so down to earth. Women like her shouldn't come to rituals. She makes Fay uncomfortable. Fay doesn't like Margaret's meditations either. Any woman who can visualize killing her own mother and enjoying it must have problems.
"Mindy's on the phone. An important call. We're to carry on without her," says Margaret snapping off the light and banging her pot lids together. Fay tinkles her triangle and visualizes a yellow globe somewhere above her left shoulder. Jodie begins wailing, deep and throaty and the hairs on Fay's arms quiver. Some of the women start swaying, raising their arms above their heads, others begin to dance, moving slowly so that they don't trip over things and each other in the darkness.
Margaret stops banging pot lids and turns on the light. "Well, that's enough for me. If Mindy's going to be on the phone all night I certainly don't intend waiting for her." Margaret leaves the room. She calls goodnight to Mindy and the front door shuts.
"I always knew she wasn't serious," says the green spring maiden with weeds in her hair "she's the only one that didn't wear a solstice gown."
"Maybe she's not into dresses," says Jodie smiling at Fay. "Anyway we could be starting our cone of power. I think that comes next."
"Not without Mindy, it's too dangerous," says careful June, placing her spoons on the bench behind her.
A shrill tuneless sound floats down the hallway. Jodie turns off the light. Fay waits for her fingers to find her robe again. She tingles her triangle with vigour and hums through vibrating lips. As the sounds increase in volume then fade Mindy's voice rises out of the darkness.
"May the circle we have formed not be broken."
Fay feels a sense of pride. She is a true ritual woman. She will never break the circle.

Fran Marno

Katherine's Thigh

Blessed be the Lord God of Israel. Pamela is fifteen and a little bit in love with the minister. All the girls are. She learns the Benedictus off by heart. The minister's wife is pale and quiet and always stands behind him. She makes the cakes and pours the tea at the communion class.
Blessed be the Lord of Israel for he hath visited and redeemed his people. The minister holds Pamela's hand a fraction too long when he says goodnight. All the girls like saying goodnight to the minister. His wife is in the kitchen doing the dishes.

Pamela is 34 and doesn't believe in God or redemption.
"Blessed be," chants Miranda.
"Blessed be," sings Miranda. "Some of you will have difficulty with these words," she pauses and smiles at the women sitting around her, " but they're very old," she says, "and come from our own women's tradition."
Pamela has no intention of chanting blessed be. "I don't like it," she tells the group, "I'm not chanting blessed be for any ritual, feminist or not."
Miranda looks at Pamela. "Never mind," she says, "we'll chant and you join in if you can. It is a women's chant," and her smile hovers expectantly over Pamela's petulant silence.

O God make clean our hearts within us.
Pamela loves the sound of the minister's voice. She fears for her heart. He might see in and guess.
And take not thy holy spirit from us.
She holds her book of common prayer in front of her and chants her response.
The minister's eyes are shut.

Pamela watches the women chanting, praying, calling to the Goddess. Some are breathy and glassy eyed, some whisper reverently, and one or two look sullen and the words slip sideways out of their mouths. Miranda is radiant. Her voice rises higher and higher. Her body lightens and lifts up and up. It suspends above the glowing circle and smiles benignly down.
"I am Miranda and you are wondrous," she sings.
"You are Miranda and You are wondrous," the women refrain.
"You are women and you are wondrous," chants Miranda.
"We are women and we are wondrous."
"Blessed be."
"Blessed be," the voices rise and sway up to the ceiling.

Pamela watches. They're serious. It's not that she's cynical but aren't they overdoing it, just a bit? She waits, stifling a yawn by clenching her teeth and spreading her nostrils. The euphoria subsides. Katherine is looking at her and winks. Pamela looks away confused. Miranda is passing energy around the circle. Pamela feels the flow as her hand is squeezed and she passes the squeeze on. She can cope with this. Something physical and pragmatic.

She never knows with the minister. Sometimes his eyes search through her heart and she feels naked before him.She dreams of him blessing her body and offering it to God. Other times he smiles and nods and passes her by and she wonders why she bothers with church at all.
The women are watching Miranda. She has her eyes shut and sways gently backwards and forwards. She stops. "Make yourself comfortable," she says, "lie down, rest against cushions, whatever feels right for you. Close your eyes."

The women wriggle and shuffle and make room for each other. Pamela lies on her stomach on the carpet with her eyes closed and breathes rhythmically. She waits for the visions to start. She's going to have a vision. She's been looking forward to this part. She's relaxed and waiting for a symbol to present itself. Miranda says it will. "Don't look for it," she says, "just relax and wait for it to present itself to you." Pamela waits. Her nostrils are full of carpet fluff. She starts sneezing. The vision doesn't come. She hears the gentle rhythmical breathing of Katherine. She can feel Katherine's thigh against hers. She wonders if Katherine knows about this.

Miranda is bringing them back into the room. "By the time I've counted to ten, have your eyes open and sit up slowly."
Pamela counts to ten and opens her eyes. Katherine is still breathing beside her. She's snoring.
"Wake up," Pamela whispers, nudging Katherine gently.
Katherine groans. "Piss off," she says.

Pamela sees the minister years later. She's heard he's had a heart attack. She goes to his church and watches a young minister take the service. At the end of the service Pamela's minister stands and blesses the congregation. He shakes hands with her as she leaves the church. "God go with you," he says. She doesn't ask him if he remembers her.

Pamela doesn't join the advanced ritual group. She meets Katherine a few years later at South City Girls. She has a feeling that she has lain naked next to her and that Katherine has seen into her heart.
"Miranda's, we met at Miranda's," she says, "remember? you fell asleep. You were snoring. You didn't want to be woken. Remember?" she says.
Katherine lifts her hand and touches Pamela gently on the cheek.
"Blessed be," she says.

Fran Marno

Seen In Auckland

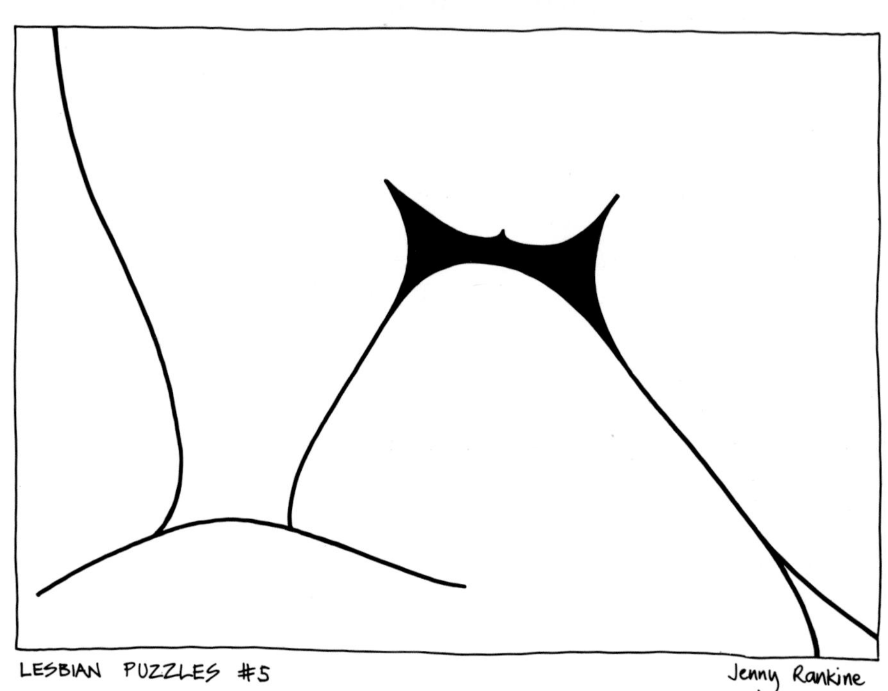

LESBIAN PUZZLES #5

Jenny Rankine

No More Self Defence At The Taihape Hall

There once lived far away in Taihape
A young woman, Sara Martha Maree
She had a Mum, a Dad and a brother,
Her life - she knew no other
She thought she would work and she did indeed
Until it was time to marry and breed.
Then alone, no encouragement at all
Sara Martha Maree went to the Taihape hall.

She listened, she kicked, she yelled - no pretence
In the name of safety and self defence.

Soon after that she began to change
Sara Martha Maree became terribly strange,
Her parents they wept and then they wailed
"Oh Where! Oh Where have we failed!"
The town all cried, "How could it be!"
A sweet young thing like Sara Martha Maree.

She said "Piss-off" to her husband-to-be
She kisses women on the lips - shamelessly,
She's cut off her hair - she thinks she's strong
She's changed her name she's had all along
Now she's Sappho Oaktree Birdsong!

There's a moral to this story - so listen carefully
Those witches, those teachers, they pervert young girls
With their fresh young faces and golden curls,
Like poor young Sara Martha Maree!
They extinguish their natural femine fear
And turn them unnatural, man-like and queer.

They must be banished all over the land
Before it gets totally out of hand
All our good women might answer the call
So no more self-defence in the Taihape hall.

Marigold

Is that all you ever think about – your stomach?

NEW LESBIAN LITERATURE 1980-88
NEW LESBIAN LITERATURE 1980-88

NEW LESBIAN LITERATURE 1980-88